The Best

DISTRIBUTION SALES BOOK EVER!

Joseph C. Ellers

N·A·W
Institute for
DISTRIBUTION
EXCELLENCE

N · A · W

Institute for

DISTRIBUTION
EXCELLENCE

About NAW and the NAW Institute for Distribution Excellence

The National Association of Wholesaler-Distributors (NAW) was created in 1946 to deal with issues of interest to the entire merchant wholesale distribution industry, thereby freeing affiliated associations to concentrate on the concerns specific to their lines of trade. NAW is a federation of more than 100 wholesale distribution associations and thousands of individual firms that collectively total more than 40,000 companies.

The role of the NAW Institute for Distribution Excellence (formerly the Distribution Research and Education Foundation) is to sponsor and disseminate research into strategic management issues affecting the wholesale distribution industry. The NAW Institute for Distribution Excellence aims to help merchant wholesaler-distributors remain the most effective and efficient channel in distribution.

ISBN 1-934014-17-6

NAW Institute for Distribution Excellence

202.872.0885

www.nawpubs.org

Contents

Acknowledgments

Writing a book is relatively easy—if you have something to say. Having something to say is the hard part. Over the years, I have been blessed with wisdom and advice from many people. These people have given me the direction that I needed to be successful in the most exciting profession in the world—professional selling.

When you start to thank people, it gets a little tough because you don't want to leave anyone out. So, I'll start with a general thank-you to all the pros with whom I have interacted over the years. There's a bunch of you, in a lot of different industries. Some of you were fairly junior when we met, but you taught me something—and I'm grateful.

A few specific thank-yous: The entire gang at Systems & Services. First, there are Nat Cain and Guerry Burnett, the great owners and teachers, who started my sales career. The late, great Bob Altier, and Greg Fair and Dan Tyner—all of them were very helpful to a green kid with a desire to sell.

My mentor Dick Russell and his son Grant showed me things about how the world works, and I will be forever in their debt for their friendship. The same goes for my friend and former business partner Art Zucker: Z-Man, you're the greatest and you've taught me life lessons as well as business lessons.

In my company, Palmetto Associates, I've also had the opportunity to work with a lot of great people who have inspired and taught me. Most important of these is Paul Clipp—a manufacturing whiz and truly one of the smartest people I've ever met. Matt Daniel and Jackie Reid also come in for some kudos. Thank-you also to Anne Copeland: You've done a lot to make this possible by doing other things so I could do what I needed to do on this project.

Although they did not impact this book specifically, the people of my hometown, Clemson, South Carolina, need a word of thanks. Clemson is a great place to grow up because there are people here who not only know a lot of things, but also are willing to share them enthusiastically with others...even kids. Thank you a million times for all that you've done to help me and a lot of others.

I also would like to thank NAW.

NAW Institute for Distribution Excellence
Board of Directors and Officers

A Few Words about the Following Words

The best way to learn is to do. The next best way is to read about things that you can do. That's what this project is all about. There are 11 chapters in the book. They are designed to be read in order. Don't be in a hurry to flip through the earlier chapters to find out the socko ending. (The world is saved, and the hero gets the girl, and all live happily ever after—with 2.4 children and a Volvo.)

The difficulty with a book on selling is that it's like a book on golf—it looks simple enough on paper, but when you get a club in your hands,...To address this issue, I have tried to make the learning experiential. Every chapter has a set of preliminary questions. You need to answer these, not just read them, before you read the chapter because they dramatically increase the value of the chapter. There also are assignments at the end of each chapter. They are designed to help you apply what you've learned. People have a tendency to get into ruts— both good ruts and bad (and bad ones always are easier). The follow-up assignments at the ends of the chapters will help you establish a few new, good habits.

The best way to use this book is to read it through from cover to cover first. (Don't even stop for snacks.) Then go back and reread chapters 2 through 11, this time answering the preliminary questions and completing the assignments at the ends of the chapters. I suggest that you take a *full month* to complete each chapter. That will help you really drive your learning process. If you want to put some afterburners on your learning, work through the book with at least one of your colleagues, or get your manager involved. Get together for a few minutes at all three stages of each chapter: Discuss your answers to the preliminary questions. Discuss the chapter. (Tell each other how it really doesn't apply to your jobs. Then humbly rethink that, and talk about how you can make it work for you.) Finally, before you move on to the next chapter, discuss how your follow-up assignments worked out. When you share with others, you put more pressure on yourself to get value, and you always get value from the input of other dedicated distributor sales pros.

Briefly, the chapters cover the distributor sales job from soup to nuts. I start with the obligatory introductory chapter, where I challenge you to begin thinking about what you "know" to be true about selling. After this bit of cerebrating, we get down to the more tactical aspects and nine basic rules of distributor sales.

Chapter 2 deals with the planning process. Successful salespeople have a plan, and I give you some questions to answer and a few tools that will help you develop a very clear plan that's designed to drive your success.

Chapter 3 works on the most critical distributor sales question: Why should the prospect switch from an existing distributor and start buying from me? Here we work on your value proposition and help you apply it to what the customer is trying to accomplish.

Chapter 4 is an overview of the distributor sales process, presented from two different views: what's going on with the customer and what needs to be happening from the salesperson's perspective. Here you are introduced to the concepts of total acquisition cost and per-unit cost, and you get an overview of the six-step sales process.

Chapters 5, 6, and 7 are a deep dive into the six-step sales process. In each chapter, you'll look at two steps and learn not only what to do, but also how to do it.

Chapter 8 focuses on the distributor sales call. Sales calls should be process driven, and in this chapter you'll see the process and learn how to diagnose when you're not adding enough value to get quality sales appointments.

Chapter 9 deals with time management. You know that the most precious thing you have is your time, so your goal should be to convert time into happiness. In your personal life, happiness is made up of time spent with your loved ones and time spent doing things to help humankind. When you get to work, you need to convert your time in sales. The primary focus of the chapter is on your professional side, but you'll pick up a few tips to help make the personal side better, too.

Chapter 10 deals with your favorite topic—you. We finally get to the personality part of selling here, and you'll find some tips on modifying your communication style to be more effective with a larger group of people.

Chapter 11 deals with presentations. You have to make them all of the time, so here you'll find a process to make them easier and more effective.

Take the time to do the work in each chapter. Spend enough time answering the preliminary questions and completing the assignments to do it right. Lao-tzu correctly stated that the journey of a thousand miles begins with one step. Each day, move at least a single step closer to distributor sales mastery.

Good selling!

The Obligatory Introductory Chapter

Before you begin, answer these questions:
1. What are the sales rules, as you now know them?
2. What are the rules that are working consciously, unconsciously, and subconsciously to control your days?

The times, they are a-changin'. The first thing you need to know about distribution sales is that you need to forget a lot of what you already have learned. Selling has been around for a long time—with few changes from the beginning until very recently. The original salespeople were known as "drummers." A person with something to sell came into the town square and beat on a drum to attract attention. From there, the profession progressed to peddlers—itinerants who went from town to town without the drum. In the early days, a lot of it was about the "show." They literally were selling the sizzle—not always the steak. From there, the relationship part of selling remained as the critical aspect until now.

Don't get me wrong. Relationship will always be part of selling. People would rather do business with people they like. But there are some key changes to distribution sales. One of the most important is the need to get back to the "proactive bias" of selling. From the end of World War II at least until the mid-1970s, the United States (and, to a lesser extent, most of the industrial nations) had it pretty good. The world had a pent-up demand for almost everything. This meant that "selling" looked a lot like "order taking." The bad news is that a huge number of people in business management and sales management positions—and a few dinosaurs still selling—have this order-taking mentality at the root of their approach. The underlying assumption is that you simply need to get out there and make friends to get an order.

There are lots of things wrong with that assumption. First, there are just not as many orders to go around as there used to be. If you're selling in the industrial sector, you might have noticed there are fewer customers. Entire industries (textiles and furniture, for example) are almost completely gone. This has happened throughout the channels served by wholesale distribution. And many of the organizations that remain are smaller than the businesses they replaced. These smaller, niche marketers are likely to remain, but they'll be buying smaller quantities.

Another factor is the change in the organizational decision-making process. For years, "good old Charley" made the decisions. Now, good old Charley has to run things past "not-quite-so-good young Bill" and "Sally, who-you-didn't-even-know-existed." The reasons are complex, but they include the fact that people now have more responsibility and often are less knowledgeable about what they're buying. The buying and selling of companies as a way to make money (rather than the buying and selling of products/services) also has forced organizations to make different kinds of decisions. These factors don't even address the advent of purchasing approaches such as vendor-managed inventory, Internet options, and integrated supply, which seek to make every purchasing decision into part of a global purchasing solution.

For another thing, there is a lot more competition—and a lot of it comes from places where they can make things cheaply. This has fueled one of the major differences in selling—the importance of price. My description of this is the "Wal-Martization" of America. Many people believe they're supposed to get things cheaply. The concept of "value" has suffered during this change. Salespeople who have not learned to sell the value of their products and services have had tough going because knowing their customer's birthdays and talking about sports just doesn't get them the order over a cheaper competitor.

The final difference in selling is an aspect that is inherent to the wholesale distribution sales profession: maybe you haven't noticed it, *but we all sell the same thing*. There are salespeople who sell products that may be similar but at least are made by different people, and they have some slight differentiation in product features. When you're a distribution salesperson, however, you're selling what everyone else is selling. If there ever was any exclusivity, there is almost none now. This makes the job of a wholesale distribution sales professional even harder than the sales job done by other salespeople.

There you have it. You know what it was and what it is. So what can you do about it? To help you in your journey, there are a few key concepts that you should take with you. These are the nine rules of selling.

Rule 1: Sell, Don't Take Orders

The point already has been made that a successful distribution salesperson sells. Sounds simple enough, but there are lots of specific activities that go along with this. A sales pro doesn't wait for the phone to ring—ever. A lot of distribution salespeople have been spoiled over the years because the phone does ring. Customers and prospects call and ask for information or quotes on a variety of products. Great. Hope it continues. What if it doesn't?

You don't want to have your success depend on whether someone else takes action. You want to be in control—or, at least, you want to be doing activities that enhance your ability to get an order. This means that you need to be working constantly to find new customers. Don't wait for them to find you. You also should be looking constantly for new people. People control opportunities; and if you get to know a few more people over the course of the year, you'll get a look at more opportunities. The most important selling behavior is understanding that opportunities come in three flavors: those the customer brings you, those you find, and those you create.

The lowest level of selling is working only on opportunities that the customer brings you. When you have good customers, they'll bring you things on which to work. They have done all of the heavy lifting: they found the problem, defined the problem, defined the solution, and are giving you a chance to help them.

The first level of proactivity is to *find* an opportunity. This requires you to make outbound calls and to talk with people who actually may have a piece of business. In these cases, the customer may have found the problem, but you at least have the possibility of helping the customer define it and maybe of defining your product/service as the solution. And because you're there, you get a chance to work on it when you might not have had the chance if you weren't in contact with the customer.

The highest level of professional selling is to *create* an opportunity. In this case, you hypothesize a problem and help the customer find it. You actually are helping customers solve problems they didn't even know they had. Here you do all the heavy lifting: you find the problem, define it, define the solution—and because you're there, you definitely are going to be part of the sale. This doesn't mean that you get the order, but your chances of getting it (at a good margin) are the highest of any of the sales options.

Think about the opportunities that you currently are working, and see how much of your business falls into each of these categories: (1) custom - er brings the opportunity, (2) you find a sales opportunity, and (3) you create an opportunity. Over the next year, try to get as much of your business as possible into the "create an opportunity" category.

Selling requires you to make things happen, not let things happen. Make sure you always are looking for chances to be proactive.

Rule 2: Selling Is about Customers, Not Orders

For distribution salespeople, the sale is neither the beginning nor the end—it's supposed to be part of the relationship. Some salespeople have the luxury of making a sale that stands alone. If you're selling multimillion-dollar capital items, you might only get to sell one of those to a customer every three or four years. In between, there may be only a minimum amount of contact with the customer. (The same holds true for selling cars, which, coincidentally, is where a lot of sales lore and training comes from because car salespeople were among the first to be formally trained.)

In distribution, you cannot simply make a sale. Each sale is part of a relationship with the customer. To that end, every sale either strengthens or weakens the relationship with the customer. Even *trying* to make a sale has the ability to help or hurt you. For example, if you present a product that the customer has no interest in, you make it harder to get to talk with that person in the future. On the flipside, a product presentation of value—even if you don't get the order—may make a customer think of you the next time something is needed.

As you are putting together your sales plan, ask yourself these questions: Will this call strengthen or hurt my relationship with the customer? Am I wasting the customer's time with this call? If you think that you may be doing that, figure out how to modify the call or presentation so that you take that particular curse off of the call.

Rule 3: Selling Is a Science (and an Art Form)

The value of the relationship (your sparkling personality) already has been confirmed. Don't let your understanding of selling stop there. The good news about personality is that most salespeople have the sort of personality that appeals to some portion of the customer base. The bad news is that most salespeople have the sort of personality that appeals *only* to some portion of the customer base. If you rely strictly on personality, you'll miss a lot of business where your personality doesn't mesh with that of the customer.

Professional salespeople also work the science (process) side of selling. One of the fundamental concepts that you will learn here is the distribution sales process. There are steps that you can follow—and the use of these steps will increase your effectiveness greatly. The benefits of using the process side of selling over the personality side are obvious. If selling is strictly an art form, then you're either born with the "artistic" talent for sales or you aren't—and there's nothing (including this fine book) that can help you. By using the process side of selling, you're acknowledging that there are things that can be learned and improved over time.

Another benefit to the process side of selling is that you can get some real "diagnostics" on where you can improve. If you approach selling as a random series of activities, you will not get any insight into what's working and what isn't. The process approach will enable you to determine where each opportunity is in the process and what your conversion rates are at each step. A practical example of this would be something as simple as your closing ratio: You might close 40% of your quotes and assume that

9

the only way to improve this is to work on your closing skills. Reviewing the process, however, might show that you lose fully half of the sales you work on because you're not dealing with the right person or because the opportunity simply was not real for you. (More about those things later.) By understanding the steps that make up the sales process, you can make more money—with less effort—because you'll know what's really working and where the real problems are with your approach.

Rule 4: Use Questions, Not Statements, Whenever Possible

From the earliest days of the drummer, selling has been focused on what you say to the customer or prospect. This carries a real burden: You have to be a good speaker. You're expected to make a series of compelling arguments that move the customer's mind from where it starts to where you want it to go. Not bad if you can do it, but what if you're not the greatest speaker? What if you don't have the compelling argument on the tip of your tongue for every issue that might arise?

The good news is that two of the more recent recognitions in selling are the power (and value) of asking questions. Think about this from the standpoint of "mind control." That's an obnoxious topic because a lot of people equate mind control with manipulation. Good distribution salespeople do not manipulate the customer because, although doing so might get an order, it almost never gets a customer. But the salesperson has to get the customer to think about the problem in a different light, if the salesperson wants the customer to place an order. To do this, the salesperson has to get the customer to think about things in a specific way. The salesperson does this by asking the right questions.

Think about it this way: While you're speaking, you assume that the customer is hanging on every word and being persuaded by the power of your arguments. In reality, the customer may be thinking about a recent fight with a spouse or about planning a vacation. The sad fact is that, while you're talking, the customer can think about any topic.

There is only one time in the discussion when you are (fairly) certain about what the customer is thinking: it's when you ask a question. In asking a question, you move the customer's mind to where you want it to be. You may not get a straight answer to a question, but at least you know that the customer is thinking about the topic you want. (There are people who can think about something else while they're speaking, but those people are few and far between. For the most part, the mind accompanies the tongue.) This means that a salesperson comes to every discussion armed with a series of questions. Questions can be used to uncover opportunities and to respond to objections.

Be careful about asking some types of questions. There are certain questions (often suggested by sales trainers) that insult the customer's intelligence. An example would be the question, Are you interested in saving money? This question is absurd and never should be asked. You could rephrase it, however. What is your goal for reducing rework? is a good question because it assumes that the customer wants to reduce rework, and it forces the customer to start thinking about a topic that you want considered.

When you're talking with customers, spend less time preparing for the brilliance that you want to impart and more time thinking about the questions that you need to ask to get the customer to think about the topics that are likely to result in an opportunity for you.

Rule 5: Create Real Sales Power for Yourself

There is too much fear-based selling. Fear-based selling is at the root of the following comments: "I can't say that to the customer" and "If I push them too hard, I'll ruin the relationship." There are times when those are the right statements, but a competent distribution salesperson doesn't have too many things in these categories because these comments dramatically inhibit your effectiveness.

Although you never should deliberately say something you think the customer won't like, you have an obligation to have "real" conversations. This means that there will be times when "tough love" is required, either to get the order or to avoid wasting time. To be empowered to do this, you have to keep the following formula in mind:

Real sales power = Opportunities in excess of need

Simple, but powerful. Think of this in the context of a job interview scenario. Assume that there are 15 companies trying to hire you. How much power do you have in this case? Tons. You can negotiate with your preferred employer and walk away from a bad offer because you have more offers than you need. The flipside would be a case where you and 14 of the best salespeople in your area are applying for the one good sales job. How much power do you have here? Not much. The employer is going to make a good hiring decision, no matter who is hired. The employer has the options, and in negotiations can play one of you against another.

Consider the sales implications: Assume that you have a sales goal of $1 million for the year. Assume further that you close 50% of your opportunities. In this scenario, anything less than $2 million in opportunities puts you in a very bad place. You have to accept almost any offer you get from any customer—even a ridiculously low price or unacceptable terms—to hit your budget.

Even at $2 million in opportunities, you have no real power relative to the market. When you get over $2 million in opportunities, you begin to have power. Think about how much strength you would have in negotiating with customers if you had $2,500,000 in opportunities. You would have $500,000 worth of opportunities that you didn't need. This would enable you to say "no" (very nicely) to customers who wanted to pay low prices or who wanted additional warranties or free shipping.

The really interesting thing about the ability to say "no" is that you often end up getting the order anyway. Customers have to ask you for something extra; if you can't give it (and you say so), they often end up buying anyway. They probably were satisfied with your original offer and merely were asking to see if you'd move off of your number. So, in a case like this, you probably win in two ways: you increase your sales power, and you get more sales than you need.

Rule 6: Know Your Disaster Index and Do Something about It

As a salesperson, you really are running a business within a business. Often, you're so good at dealing with certain customers that you get more and more of their business. At some point, you have a vague feeling of nausea because so much of your business is dependent on a few customers. The same thing can happen with product sales. You're so good at selling some products that they are responsible for a large percentage of your sales.

The first thing you should do is calculate your "disaster index." It's simple. Take the total sales of your largest customer and divide it by your total sales. Here's an example: ABC Company bought $300,000 from you last year, and your total sales were $1 million. ABC Company represents 30% of your total sales. You also need to look at the issue from the standpoint of your total sales to one industry. Do the calculation using not just your best customer, but also your largest market segment. For example, if you sold 80% of your products to commercial contractors, that percentage of your total sales number would be 80%, not 30%. This is because an industry-wide issue, such as a recession, would impact all of those types of customers, not just the largest.

Next, take the total sales of your largest product (product group) and divide that number by your total sales. Here's an example: You sold $250,000 of XYZ widgets to your customer base. This represents 25% of your total sales of $1 million.

Now, multiply the two numbers together: 30% x 25% = 7.5%; 7.5% of $1 million = $75,000 in potential risk. In this case, the salesperson has about $75,000 worth of extreme risk in the territory. The salesperson can expect to lose this amount of business in a given year. (In this case, 7.5% is not a very large amount; but if your number is 20%–30% instead of 7.5%, you may have real issues about the health of your territory.)

When you have identified your disaster index, the next thing is to do something about it. You can see that the two things you could do to lessen the index would be to

- sell more to other customers
- sell a wider range of products to your customers.

The goal is to lessen the number—neither by selling less to your good customer nor by selling less of your good products, but by selling more of other products to other customers.

Rule 7: Focus on Activities; Results Will Follow

We know that sales is a numbers game. If two salespeople are relatively equal in skill level, and one makes 5 calls a week while the other makes 10, the odds are that the salesperson who makes 10 calls will sell more than the one who makes only 5. There even are instances when the salesperson who makes more calls sells more than the salesperson who has better skills but makes fewer calls. The raging battle within the sales community revolves around the question of quantity versus quality. The best distribution salespeople do enough of the right activities in the right ways to make sales. But there are lots of salespeople getting good results who do enough of the right activities in a less-than-right way.

The suggestion here is not to do a lot of sales stuff poorly. The suggestion is to focus on activities, not on results. Too many salespeople review only their results ("I'm at 105% of goal"), rather than also looking at their activities ("I made enough sales calls this week to be successful").

For your self-management efforts, set up some specific activity goals, and hold yourself accountable. How many total sales calls should you make in an average week? How many of those should be on existing customers? How many on new prospects? How many sales presentations should you give for specific products over the course of a month? How many demonstrations? How many samples? How many new opportunities should you find in a month? How many quotes should you issue? For how many dollars?

Notice in that list that you have not been asked to think about results. The fact is that you cannot control results. The customer has a lot to say about how much you end up selling. But you have a lot to say about how much effort you put into trying to sell the customer. Focus on the things that you can control—your activities—and the results (most often) will take care of themselves. (It wouldn't hurt to improve the quality of your efforts, too.)

Rule 8: Three Things Really Matter

In sales, there are three things that really matter: finding customers, finding people, and finding opportunities.

Finding Customers

The first thing that matters is finding new customers. Over time, you're going to lose some customers, and there's nothing that you can do about it. They will go out of business or relocate, or some corporate guy will decide to buy everything from China. That's the breaks of selling. Your goal is always to have some new customers working. A good analysis for you (if you have been selling for a while) is to look at your top 10 customers of five years ago and compare their sales numbers to what you sold them last year. Do you have any new customers in your top 10? What happened to the sales numbers for your previous 10? Did some of them decline or disappear altogether? Understand the impact this has on your business, and work proactively to have some new customers in your personal pipeline at all times.

Finding People

The second thing that matters is finding new people. This is not the same thing as finding new customers. You can find new people inside your existing accounts as well as new people in new customers. People = Opportunities. That simple sales equation should guide your efforts to find new people. There are some products that you won't be able to sell to your existing customers unless you find some other people inside that business who need those products. You'll lose some pieces of business because you haven't found the right people to help protect your business. You'll miss early warning signals about your competitor's presence in some of your key accounts because you don't have the right contacts.

Make it a point always to be looking for new people who can help you. People may be categorized in the following manner:

- **Sole decision makers** make decisions without approval from others.

- **Joint decision makers** make decisions with input/approval from others.

- **Recommenders and influencers** strongly influence the buying decisions.

- **Information gatherers** just gather information and pass it along.

- **Time wasters.**

It's sad that they tend not to have those labels listed on their name tags. Your goal is to identify as many of the relevant people as you can within your customers' (and prospects') organizations.

Finding Opportunities

This is where the sale originates. Every day, you should find (or create) at least one piece of business on which to work. A day without a new opportunity is a bad day for a salesperson. Take stock of your sales days. How many days pass without finding a specific piece of business that you have a chance of booking?

Rule 9: Isaac Rules

Think back to your high-school science class, and you may be able to remember this law from Sir Isaac Newton: *An object at rest tends to remain at rest unless acted on by an outside force. An object in motion tends to remain in motion, along the same line, unless acted on by an outside force.* How is that relevant to sales? you may be thinking.

Here's how: Selling is simple in process but difficult in execution because it seeks to counter this law of the universe. By understanding the law, you know that a customer who never has bought from you is likely to continue never buying from you, and a customer who has bought some things but not others is likely to continue that pattern. Even worse, the law rules the behaviors of individuals. You have been successful with certain customers and certain products because you sold in a specific way. That success has made it very likely that you will continue to sell that way throughout your career. But what happens if the situation changes, as it does on a regular basis? You have to change with it, and that's really tough for most people.

If you were to videotape a few days in the life of just about anyone, you'd see that the days are very similar. The person gets up at the same time and goes through the same ritual to get to work every day. The person follows a similar pattern at work—from the first cup of coffee until the end of the day. These patterns are necessary and help us get through our days efficiently. The bad news is that bad habits are hard to break. The dessert you always have on Friday and the beer you have when you get home from work are fine until the habit becomes dessert after every meal and six beers before dinner every evening.

The same holds true for your patterns of selling. Going into your office before making the first call of the day or coming back to the office at 3:30

are fine occasionally; but when they become habits, they hurt your ability to have the success you want your sales career to provide.

To be effective, you have to be able to change. Change requires first understanding what you're doing and then making a conscious decision to modify the behavior over a time period long enough for the changed behavior to become the new habit. The bad news is that it generally takes longer to establish a good habit than a bad one. Think about it: adding dessert to your meal is always easier than getting to the gym four days a week.

Everything tends to remain as it has been, *unless acted on by an outside force.* The outside force is you, the sales professional. To what activity do you need to apply force to change a behavior, to change a result?

Conclusion

In this chapter, I have tried to present the key rules of selling, as they exist today. As with all rules, there are times when they need to be broken; and not every rule applies all the time. Remember, however, that you need to live your professional life based on the rules, not the exceptions. Not every bear you stumble across in the woods will kill you, but avoiding bears is still a good idea. Try to follow the rules and make conscious decisions to break them when the circumstances dictate.

FOLLOW-UP ASSIGNMENTS

1. Review your answers to the questions at the beginning of the chapter. See how many of them are in agreement with what you've read in the chapter. See how many are in conflict.

2. Do a proactivity assessment to determine how many of your current opportunities fall into each of these categories:
   - opportunities brought to you by the customer
   - opportunities you found
   - opportunities you created.

3. List your current "activity" goals (for example, 12 scheduled sales appointments per week).

4. List three to five questions you should ask to uncover an opportunity for your most important focus product.

5. Calculate your close ratio for last year: How much did you quote? How much did you close? What's still open from last year? Subtract the open quotes from total quotes, and divide the sold quotes by the remainder. Here's an example: Quoted, $2 million. Still open from last year, $500,000. Last year's sales, $1 million. $1,000,000 ÷ $1,500,000 = 66%.

6. Calculate your disaster index: Sales to top customer or market x sales of top product or product group.

7. What are you doing to "create your own economy"? What are your numbers for each of these elements this year:
   - new customers called on?
   - new people called on?
   - new opportunities identified?

Have an Activity-Based Sales Plan—and Work It

Before you begin, answer these questions:

1. What do you want to sell?
2. To whom do you want to sell?
3. What does a good order look like?
4. How many scheduled sales calls should you make in an average week?
5. What percent of your sales should come from existing customers? From new customers?
6. What percent of your sales should come from existing products? From new products?
7. How clear are you on the following:
   - products you need to defend with specific customers?
   - products you need to introduce to specific customers?
   - products you need to grow at specific accounts?
   - products for which you need to define the potential?
   - products you just need to forget about with specific customers—for now?

Too many sales plans are just numbers. Even planning tools like quotas don't really do the job. Top-level distribution sales pros have activity-based goals that drive daily behaviors. As you thought about the questions at the start of the chapter, how comfortable did you feel with your answers? The more vague they were, the less likely you are to have a clear understanding of what you want to accomplish.

Professional selling has good time management at its base. This means that you start every day with a specific list of things planned that will help you achieve your sales goals. Your goal would be to spend as much of every day as possible doing the things that are most important. If you could not easily answer the questions above, you can't even review what you have done because there is nothing concrete to compare what you did with what you wanted to do.

An age-old argument within the sales community involves this question: Do you want me to fill out reports or sell? You need to spend as much time as you can selling—but think about how much more effective you'll be if you're doing the right things. For many of you, this chapter will be like going to the dentist. You won't like it, but the end result will be better for you than not doing it.

The Four Key Questions

Start with being very clear about what you (really) are trying to accomplish on a daily basis: You're making sales calls on the customers that you really want to sell to, trying to find the opportunities that are what you really want to sell, and finding opportunities that meet the definition of what a good order really looks like. Or, you're just going out there everyday hoping to stumble across some business. The choice is yours—but you get different results when you really go after something specific. To get a clear focus, begin by answering the following four key questions.

Question 1: What Do You Want to Sell?

Over the years, I have asked many distributor salespeople this question, and the number-one answer has been, "Everything we have." The bad news about that answer is that, for most of you, it means trying to sell thousands of things every day. No one is up to that task. What this answer really means is that the salesperson doesn't have a focus on the kinds of things he or she wants to sell. There are other answers to this question that say the same thing in different ways. Some distribution salespeople say that they want to sell "what the customer wants/needs." And sometimes the answer is that the salesperson wants to sell the company (better ask the owner) or themselves. All of those answers have some truth in them, but those are not the answers that the top-level pros give.

The best distribution salespeople answer the questions in the following way: "My goal is to sell the following products (*A, B,* and *C*). Last month,

I was focusing on these products (*D, E,* and *F*). Probably next quarter, I will be focused on selling the following products (*G, H,* and *I*)." The best salespeople have a very clear picture of the products that they're promoting. It makes sense that if you go out to the field looking to sell certain things, you are more likely to sell them.

The assignment that you have in this section is to put together a list of "focus" products or product groups that you want to focus on selling. Your next step is to give this list to your boss and see if there is agreement. In an ideal situation, you already know these products because your management has taken the time to tell you what they are; and your company's training, activities, and compensation plans support the effort. If management hasn't done that, take a leadership position and put the list together.

Now you have some specific things that you can hold yourself accountable for as you set up sales calls.

Question 2: To Whom Do You Want to Sell?

Again, when this question has been asked, the most frequent answer is, "Everyone," or some version of that answer. Again, that answer is partly true. You certainly would take an order from anyone who would like to give you one. But the answer is not nearly good enough for the distribution sales pro. Sales pros give a different kind of answer.

When asked, their answers sound like this: "I spend as much of my time as possible with accounts that look like this: they are locally owned businesses of between $25 and $30 million in sales, in the food, power, and solid waste disposal industries." You need to fill in your own details here; but note that, again, the best distribution salespeople are very specific about the people with whom they're trying to spend time.

The answer to this question should be driven by the following factors:

- **The answer to what you want to sell**—In many cases, when you answer this question, you begin to limit the accounts that you can call on because some of your accounts probably are more likely to buy some of the focus products than are others.

- **Your diversification goals**—A lot of salespeople look at their territories and decide (correctly) that their incomes are too dependent on certain customers or a certain customer segment. (Remember the disaster index.) Smart distribution sales pros pay attention to this and always are looking for ways to diversify. They do this for the following reasons: they reduce the risk of losing a lot of income if they lose a key customer or a key customer segment, they provide an economic hedge because not all customers "recess" at the same time, and they find that some prospects have not bought simply because there has been no effort.

- **The way of the world**—Too many of our customers are in some sort of economic flux. How many of your accounts might move to Mexico, China, or to other parts of the United States? You need to understand that you have the primary responsibility to protect your income, and that means actively managing your "sales investment portfolio," otherwise known as your territory.

Your assignment here looks a lot like the previous assignment. Define the characteristics of a good customer/prospect. Address the following factors as part of this assignment:

- the business they're in
- their customers
- size of the business
- your (estimated) potential
- length of time in business
- ownership
- ties to your existing customers, if any.

Again, run your answer by your boss to ensure that you're both on the same page.

Question 3: What Does a Good Order Look Like?

The most common answer is, "Any/every order." But, again, this answer does not provide the right kind of focus. The answer that the dedicated professional gives sounds like this: "A good order is $1,500 at 28%, and it includes at least four line items and repeats a minimum of 12 times per year." You should fill in your own answers to this question, but notice how specific the sample answer is. Salespeople who give answers like that can be absolutely certain on every order whether they have accomplished something "good" or just gotten an order.

You have yet another assignment: Put together your "good order" definition. Run it past your boss. Go get some.

Question 4: How Many Sales Calls Should You Make in an Average Week?

The standard answer is, "As many as I can" or something that sounds a lot like that. This answer allows salespeople never to hold themselves accountable to the most important activity target there is—the sales call quota. Smart distribution sales managers work with their teams to set goals in this area. If your manager has not done so already, you need to take a stab at it.

The answers that are good sound like this: "My goal is to make a minimum of 12 scheduled field calls per week. I supplement this with 4–6 scheduled phone appointments, and I always have a list of 10–12 customers or prospects whom I can hit with a relationship maintenance call if I have a cancellation or get a few extra minutes." An inside salesperson's answer probably would have a lot higher number of scheduled appointments because that person doesn't have to contend with issues like driving time.

This answer not only shows that the salesperson has clear goals, but also that the salesperson has an individual accountability system. You will have different answers to this question, based on what you're selling and on your territory. However, there is one statistic you need to keep in mind: normally, salespeople with more sales appointments sell more than salespeople with fewer appointments. This holds true up to about 15 appointments a week. Then the numbers start to go the other way. But if you're currently averaging 9 appointments a week, and you move the average to 11, you can count on more sales over time.

Your assignment? You guessed it: document how your week should look, and then run it past your boss.

Are you seeing a trend here? The best distribution salespeople have very specific goals that are quantifiable. They know what they want to sell and whom they want to sell to, they can define the kinds of orders they want, and they have a specific goal that relates to the building block of selling—the sales call. Start each day with a yardstick and measure yourself against it on a regular basis.

Your 3 x 3 Sales Plan

The second item to address as part of an activity-based sales plan is the way you intend to get your business. There are very few ways to get new business:

- Sell more of what you already are selling to existing customers.

- Sell new products to existing customers (either additional current products or brand-new products).

- Sell to new customers the products you currently are selling.

- Get some new products and sell them to new customers.

Ponder this for a while, and try to come up with some more....Okay, that's enough time; there aren't any. Those are your choices. To make it a little easier to understand, I've put the choices into the chart below:

Raise Prices	Existing Products	New Products
Existing Customers	1	2
New Customers	3	4

Notice that the boxes of the chart have been numbered. Each number signifies the degree of difficulty that a salesperson faces when attempting to accomplish the objective listed for the box. The lower the number, the "easier" the task, so the easiest task (box 1) would be selling more of the products that you already are selling to customers who already are buying those products from you. As an example, let's say that you currently are selling cutting tools to a machine shop, but that shop buys only 40% of the tools from you and buys the balance from other distributors. With a limited amount of effort, you may be able to increase your share to 50% in that account.

The hardest task (box 4) would be selling brand-new products to brand-new accounts. Staying with the same example, your company adds a completely new type of "green" lubricant, and you try to sell it to a brand-new account that you have identified as important because of its initiative to "go green." This would be a much tougher assignment than the one in box 1.

As you work through this process, keep in mind that two things tend to happen to your sales in box 1: they flatten out and margins decline. The way that you attack sluggish sales and declining margins is to work in boxes 2, 3, and 4. The problem is that those boxes get progressively harder to work in—but the sales professional is willing to invest the time in those boxes today for the returns received in the future.

Your assignment is to put together a 3 x 3 matrix for what you want your territory to look like. Let's walk through each of the boxes and describe not only the box, but also the reasons why you should put a goal (and your time) in that box.

Box 1: Existing Products to Existing Customers

Although none of the boxes' objectives is easy to accomplish, this is the easiest box to address. It's also possibly the most dangerous box to spend time in because of what you already have learned about how the basic laws of the universe guide the sales process. (Remember Sir Isaac Newton.)

As a distribution salesperson, you probably have an existing customer base where products are being bought. (If you're new, you inherited a territory where this is the case.) This circumstance will require attention because those customers will call in and ask for quotes, samples, demonstrations, and a fair amount of customer service—and you need to provide it. Your question is, How much time should I spend here? If you're not careful, you'll spend almost all of your time with these customers. Although you need to spend some time, there are a few questions that you need to consider:

- How much additional "good" business is here?
- Are some of my customers at risk for factors out of my control?
- Are some of the vendors that I sell to these customers at risk?
- (and the ultimate question) Will spending more time here make my territory healthier?

You do need to spend regular time with your existing customers—handling existing business—but you need to be clear on your time investment. For many salespeople, spending a lot of time on existing accounts won't yield any significant sales. And you may be in the position of having to "buy" your increased share by selling at dramatically discounted prices. That additional 10% of cutting tools may require you to lower your price on every cutting tool you sell by 10% to get the volume, and that might not be a good trade. Also keep in mind that some of your existing customers may be headed out of town for different reasons. And remember that you probably are going to lose some sales in this box every year, no matter what you do.

As you're doing your sales planning, therefore, decide how much of your existing business you think you can keep, and then budget that amount of sales. As an example, you may decide that you really only want 75% of your business next year to come from existing sales to existing customers. This decision doesn't necessarily mean that sales go down in this box, but it would require you to get 25% of your total budget in some combination of boxes 2, 3, and 4. (Hang onto the 75% number as we go forward.)

Box 2: New Products to Existing Customers

There are two different definitions for "new" in box 2. One definition is the one used earlier—selling a new line of green lubricant—but this time to an existing customer. The other definition is simply selling something you always have sold to an existing customer who never has bought it. Here the example would look like this: You're selling five different types of food service equipment to a restaurant, and the restaurant uses three additional types of equipment. You sell that additional equipment, but the restaurant never has bought any of it from you. You may have a goal of selling the restaurant at least one of those products over the next year.

With these two definitions of "new," you can decide how much of your upcoming sales budget should be in box 2. For most distribution salespeople, there is a wealth of income in this box. You already have a relationship with the customer, and often there are lots of lines you aren't selling to your existing accounts. Here's one simple analysis that you can do: Calculate the average number of lines/products that you sell to your top 10 accounts. Then look at how many lines you sell to accounts 11 to 25. In many cases, you have the ability to sell double or triple the amount of lines to your top accounts, and those are easier sales than the sales in boxes 3 and 4.

For the sake of discussion, let's say that your goal is to sell an additional 10% of your budget in box 2. (Given the goal of 75% of sales in box 1, you now have accounted for 85% of your sales goal.)

Box 3: Existing Products to New Customers

The definition for this box is simple: you are trying to sell to new customers products that you always have sold. The decision about how much effort to put here should be based on the stability of your existing customer base. If you have a stable customer base, this number could be relatively small. If you're concerned about whether your existing accounts will be around or if they're likely to move to reverse auctions in the next 12 months, you could put more sales emphasis here.

This box is where you address your need to diversify your territory. Do you want to create a more recession-proof territory? If so, put some time into the effort, and start with a firm budgeted sales number that you plan to pursue. An example of this might be your desire to increase sales to food-related customers in your territory. If they currently account for only 5% of your sales, and you know that they are more recession proof than the home builders who account for 70% of your sales, you might set a goal of selling more products to that group. For our discussion purposes, let's say you have decided on 10% for this box. (You now have accounted for 95% of your sales budget, so I guess the suspense for box 4 is kind of dulled.)

Box 4: New Products to New Customers

You already know the definition for this one. These are new products (not sold by your company before) to new accounts. Sometimes you have to do this to support a strategic vendor. Sometimes you use these products as door-openers for new accounts. Often these products have really good margins, and you need to sell them to improve the overall gross margins of your accounts. It's the toughest kind of sale because you're dealing with two new variables—the customer and the product—and the degree of difficulty goes up accordingly.

Remember the previous example of using the new line of green lubricant? This time you'll use it to open up new accounts. For the sake of this discussion, let's say that your goal for box 4 is 5%. You now have a sales plan that looks like this:

Raise Prices	Existing Products	New Products
Existing Customers	1 (75%)	2 (10%)
New Customers	3 (10%)	4 (5%)

This is a coherent overall sales plan that not only shows that you have thought about your market, but also addresses the time allocation required. At a bare minimum, you have agreed to spend 10% of your time trying to sell new things to existing customers (box 2) and 15% of your time trying to sell things to new customers (box 3 + box 4). Based on experience and observation, you probably will have to spend more than that, which means either you'll have to get more efficient in doing box 1 business or you'll have to work some overtime.

Your assignment now is to think through your territory and come up with a rational approach to how you want it to look and how much effort you need to spend to make it work like that. Again, the first cut is up to you. After you have completed your chart, take it to your manager and present it. Is there agreement? When agreement is in place, it's much easier for you to do the right thing.

The Sales Planning Matrix

The next iteration of the 3 x 3 Sales Plan is the Sales Planning Matrix. The following discussion is not for the faint of heart. It's a powerful self-management tool that absolutely will focus you on what really matters and probably will help you make a few dollars.

The matrix shown below is an abbreviated example of the full matrix. In a complete matrix, the salesperson selects eight or nine focus products or product groups. The sales rep further selects approximately 30 existing customers and another 5 or 6 key prospects for the territory. (There are exceptions, but these are the most common numbers. This number of accounts often would represent 80% of your territory potential.) The last two categories are always "Other Customers" and "Other Products." In this way, you have your entire territory on one piece of paper.

The key is not only to select the focus products (what you want to sell) and the target accounts (to whom you want to sell?), but also to put them in priority order. Lots of salespeople simply run the list of their top 30 accounts and leave them in that order. Not so fast, salesperson. That approach fails the intelligence test. Take some time to think about the ideas that we have discussed in this chapter. Are the existing accounts the ones with the most long-term potential? The safest? Note in the sample matrix presented below that one of the *prospects* is number 3 on the list— ahead of a lot of existing customers. This means that the prospect is really important and needs focused effort.

The same holds true with the products that are selected. You're not supposed merely to look at the products you sold last year. Look at the products you *should* be selling. Which ones do you need to focus on for key vendors? Which ones do you need to sell to help improve your gross margin in your territory? Which ones do you need to sell because they're door-openers for other products?

One organization located in the southeast United States relied very heavily on selling to textile and furniture manufacturers. The organization realized that the customer base was evaporating, and the management put together a Sales Planning Matrix that not only had their top customers listed as "Other Customers," but also had products with little or no sales listed as products 1–5. This sent the obvious message to the sales team members that they had a truly different year ahead of them.

Here's an abbreviated example of the Sales Planning Matrix:

	Product 1	Product 2	Product 3	Product 4	Other Products
Customer 1	10,000 10,000	5,000 14,000	15,000 13,000	0 ?	150,000 ?
Customer 2	42,000 55,000	0 10,000	12,000 13,000	500 ?	25,000 0
Prospect 3	0 ?	0 ?	0 ?	0 ?	500 ?
Customer 4	5,000 25,000	0 0	5,000 10,000	0 ?	23,000 ?
Other customers	125,000 ?	75,000 ?	35,000 ?	12,000 ?	40,000 ?

The matrix is composed of blocks. As you can see, each block has two numbers (or a number and a question mark). The top number is the actual sales dollars done for that product with that customer over the last year. The second number is the estimated potential for sales of that product to that customer. A third number that would be added in each block is the block's agreed sales target.

The simplicity of the matrix is in changing a blanket sales budget into a series of smaller budgets, each with its own strategy and action items. When you have completed the matrix, you will have a real sales plan for your territory.

The Five Basic Sales Strategies

There are only five basic sales strategies, and they can be remembered by the following initials: D, I, G, F, and F.

D = Defend. The first of the sales strategies is to *defend* the business you have. If you have all of the business in a given block (or all the business you reasonably can get), defend it. The following blocks would be candidates for the *defend* strategy:

- customer 1/product 1 (sales and potential are the same: $10,000)

- customer 1/product 3 (sales for the previous year are higher than the potential for the next year because the known usage will be less: $15,000 versus $13,000)

- customer 2/product 3 (maybe, if you decide that you reasonably cannot get the other $1,000: $12,000 versus $13,000).

Defend activities include spending time with the people who control that portion of the buy and possibly coming up with ways to link sales of that product to sales of other products that can't be matched by competitors. (One company tied the pricing of its commodity products to purchases of some noncommodity products. For example, the pricing on cutting tools remains constant if the customer purchases at least $5,000 worth of green lubricant.) Defend it if you have all you can get.

I = Introduce. To *introduce* means to begin to sell a product to an account that has not purchased it previously. The following block would be a candidate for the *introduce* strategy: customer 2/product 2 (the salesperson previously sold *nada* and has identified $10,000 of potential sales).

Introduce activities would involve identifying new people inside accounts who might control the buy, presenting samples or doing demonstrations of new products, or possibly providing references from other customers. Introduce it if you have none of it.

G = Grow. The third strategy is to *grow. This* applies to areas where you currently are getting some of the sales but there is potential to really increase them. The *grow* strategy might apply to the following boxes:

- customer 1/product 2 ($5,000 of current sales versus $14,000)

- customer 2/product 1 ($42,000 of current sales versus $55,000)

- customer 4/products 1 and 3 ($5,000 versus $25,000, and $5,000 versus $10,000, respectively).

Grow activities would include finding additional decision makers who could authorize a larger buy from one distributor or identifying and overcoming reasons why buyers do not purchase your product but do prefer other distributors. Grow it if you have some of it.

F = Find Out. The first F stands for *find out.* You're not sure how much potential exists, so you have to find out before you can decide what kind of strategy is appropriate. The *find out* strategy might apply to these boxes:

- customer 1/product 4 and other products, time permitting
- customer 2/product 4
- customer 3/every box
- customer 4/product 4 and other products, time permitting
- other customers/every box, time permitting.

For each case presented in that list, you don't know the annual potential—even if you sold those customers some products. Do not make the mistake of assuming that they bought everything they could. Sometimes customers buy something from you once simply because their normal distributor could not meet the due date.

Find out activities would involve identifying decision makers who control the spending. They also might include touring existing customers' facilities to see how they use products. If you don't know the potential, your first mission is to find out. You can't know how much time to spend trying to sell something unless you know what the payoff might be.

F = Forget about It. The second F strategy is realizing that there is nothing to be done about sales in a certain box over the coming year. There may be several different reasons for this: the customer may not buy that product or might be under a contract with a competitor that can't be broken during the coming year. The *forget about it* strategy would apply to the following boxes:

- customer 2/other products
- customer 4/product 2.

The only *forget about it* activity is filing it away for future reference. Contracts expire, and other things change. The fact that the customer cannot or will not buy from you today doesn't mean that the customer never will have a need. Forget about it if you can't sell it within the current year.

• • •

A completed matrix (completed, that is, before discovering the potentials in the *find out* categories) might look like this:

	Product 1	Product 2	Product 3	Product 4	Other Products
Customer 1	10,000 10,000 10,000	5,000 14,000 10,000	15,000 13,000 13,000	0 ?	150,000 ?
Customer 2	42,000 55,000 50,000	0 10,000 7,500	12,000 13,000 12,000	500 ?	25,000 0
Prospect 3	0 ?	0 ?	0 ?	0 ?	500 ?
Customer 4	5,000 25,000 20,000	0 0 0	5,000 10,000 7,500	0 ?	23,000 ?
Other customers	125,000 ?	75,000 ?	35,000 ?	12,000 ?	40,000 ?

As the distribution salesperson learns the potentials in the *find out* boxes, the decision might be that the appropriate strategy is *defend* or *grow* (as it might be for customer 2/product 4), *introduce* (customer 1/product 4), or *forget about it* (perhaps customer 1/box 4).

Notice that for all of the items in "Other Customers" and several of the items in "Other Products" boxes, there was a reference to "time permitting." This helps the salesperson focus on what really matters—the *defined* (target) customers and prospects and the focus products.

Conclusion

Successful selling requires a detailed plan. The bad news is that you have to stop doing and start thinking a little about what you want to accomplish. The good news is that this is something you only have to do once a year. You can allow yourself the freedom to tweak the plan quarterly, and you should review progress monthly, but the heavy lifting should be only an annual event.

FOLLOW-UP ASSIGNMENTS

1. Set a sales goal for yourself (your quota, if you have one).

2. Answer these questions:
   - What do you want to sell? (focus products)
   - To whom do you want to sell? (target account list)
   - What does a good order look like?
   - How many sales calls should you make?

3. Construct a 3 x 3 matrix to provide overall guidance for your territory.

4. Put together a Sales Planning Matrix to drive the detail.

Articulating Your Value Proposition

Before going out into the field or picking up the phone, you have to be very clear about the answer to this question: Why should I win business? Sounds simple enough, and lots of distribution salespeople answer the question simply: "Because of our quality, service, and value." The problem is that your competitors tend to use exactly the same words. The bigger problem is that those words mean almost nothing to your customers and prospects.

Winning an order requires you to offer something that the customer needs or wants and currently is not getting. If the customer buys cleaning supplies from Distributor 1, and they arrive when needed and at a relatively stable price, and the customer doesn't have any significant quality problems, what makes you think the customer is interested in buying cleaning supplies from you? You may be asked for a quote in hopes that you will low-ball the price, and the customer can extract a few pounds of flesh from the current distributor. But, in that case, you really have not demonstrated any value. To sell value, you have to have a real value proposition that's "provably different" from your competitors.

As one of your first steps, you need to perform a realistic competitive survey in your territory. Start by identifying your top three competitors. Then look at the value that those competitors truly offer. Do they sell the same products that you do, or do you offer some products/services that are different? What kinds of services do the competing companies offer? Free delivery, customer pickup options, or technical support? Then look at the value offered by the distribution salespeople against whom you compete. What are their backgrounds, education, and training? You need to understand the whole package that you are competing against so that you can identify things that you (can) do differently. Remember that you're not competing in a vacuum. The customer isn't deciding between using and not using you. Rather, the customer's decision is whether to stay with the current vendor or switch the business to you. Understand your competition—and the value they offer—so you can put together a provably different solution.

The Ultimate Sales Equation

To create your value proposition, you need to know the following sales equation:

Real sales opportunity = Product/service that you sell + *something else.*

For many salespeople, the equation looks a little different:

The prospect buys pipe = I can sell them pipe.

Wrong. To sell anything, you have to give the customer a reason to do something different. (Remember that you're trying to overcome Sir Isaac.) Customers normally want to do what they always have done. Your mission is to get them to decide that they want to do something different—which means that you have to help them see a different result. When you call on contractors who have been in business for 20 years, you're calling on people who think they know what to do to be successful. (Still in business, right?) So you have to find a way to get them to reexamine their decisions.

Professional salespeople have as many different + *something else*s as possible in their bag of tricks—and they know both when and how to use them. This means that you have to have some clearly defined value propositions that can be used in different situations.

Let's use the example of the prospect buying chemicals from Distributor 1. You work with the purchasing agent and show that the company can carry 50% less inventory because of your local stock. Over the next 90 days of working with you, the company can convert $25,000 worth of inventory into cash in hand. In this case, the sales equation looks like this:

Real sales opportunity = Chemicals + $25,000 cash over the next 90 days.

This is a + *something else* that has real provable value. To put these kinds of value propositions together, you need to have a clear understanding of what your customers might be trying to accomplish.

What Customers Really Want

In the old days, distribution salespeople were very focused on product knowledge and relationships. Both of those factors continue to have value, but they're becoming less important. To get customers to buy from you, you need to be able to come up with compelling, documented reasons for them to deal with all of the rigmarole they have to address to buy from a different distributor.

This means you must have a real understanding of the customer's business; a clear picture of how the people you're calling on are measured; and some grasp of what organizations are trying to accomplish. Some of the items listed below are more relevant when dealing with for-profit customers, but most of the items also would apply to customers such as schools, hospitals, government agencies, and religious organizations. Most organizations are trying to take cost out of what they do so they can provide more value to their customers or users. Let's take a look at the things customers and prospects probably are working on right now.

Customers Want to Sell More

For almost all commercial organizations you call on, their priority is to sell more. You need to understand how what you sell factors into that priority. There are lots of ways that you can help:

- **Reduce their costs.** When they reduce their costs, they may be able to win a few more jobs without sacrificing their margins.

- **Reduce their quote throughput.** If they can turn their quotes around faster, they might be able to win a few more jobs. What can you do to help them get their quotes out faster?

- **Enhance their products/services.** This is really about helping them create or define their competitive advantages. By using your product or service, how will they be able to differentiate themselves from their competitors?

If you can get the right people involved in this discussion, you can differentiate yourself and sell more to them. As of this moment, how clear are you on what your customers and prospects are trying to do to be able to sell more?

Customers Want to Increase Price and Improve Margins

In this big-box world we currently inhabit, all the average consumer wants to talk about is lower price. That not only causes downward price pressure on what your customers are trying to sell, but it also flows downhill right to you. A lot of your customers need to increase their prices, or they won't be able to stay in business. Are there products or services that you can sell them that will help them increase their prices to their customers? If you can help them create a differentiated product, they may be able to increase their prices.

The flipside of this discussion is about improving margins. They might be okay with the prices they're getting currently if they can reduce their costs of providing the product or service. The bad news is that they try to get you to reduce your price as part of that equation. But the price of your product may not be the problem. The issue may be more about the labor wasted in using the product than the actual cost of purchasing it.

A lot of service-type businesses use the following model: every bill should be 1/3 profit, 1/3 labor cost, and 1/3 product cost. If you can reduce the combined labor/product portion of the bill from 66% to 60%, the customer can gain an additional 6% without raising prices—and that would be a good thing, right?

Look at your customer base. How well do you understand your customers' costs? Do you know how they try to make money? What are the questions you need to ask to better understand that? Then here's the real kicker: when you get the answers, do you have some specific recommendations that will help your customers reduce their costs—something other than simply cutting the prices of what you sell them?

Customers Want to Reduce Their Inventories

Everyone has figured it out: Inventory = Real money. Your opportunity is to help your customers reduce their inventories. For every $1 million in sales that a contractor customer does, how much inventory should the contractor have? You should be able to get some industry averages for the best contractors. There's a ratio that successful ones run on—maybe more than one business model. What are the ratios? Now, what are the ratios of your customers? With which of your current customers have you worked to reduce their inventories? What happened to the profitability of their businesses? How much cash could you put back into their pockets over the next year if they worked with you?

Customers Want to Reduce Scrap, Rework, and Warranty Costs

All customers know that this is the worst money they spend. They have bought something that they end up either reworking or throwing away. Or they have to deal with a call-back from a dissatisfied customer, often paying overtime to their people to fix problems that should not have happened. Professional salespeople understand these costs for their customers. What are these costs for the most successful customers? What are they for your current customers? What projects have you been involved with in the last year in which you helped your customers reduce these costs? Are those projects documented? How much did they save?

Customers Want to Increase Throughput and Decrease Downtime

Both industrial and contractor customers are concerned about this one. For industrial customers, increased throughput means that they get more product off their lines in the same period of time. For contractor customers, this means that they install more HVAC units or rough-plumb more condos in the same time. This translates into lower operating costs, higher profits, or higher sales volumes—and sometimes all three can be assisted by this effort.

For your current customers, what kinds of goals do they have to increase their throughput or decrease their downtime? For the industry, what kinds of numbers do the best get? What kinds of results do your current customers get?

Again, back to the same old song: What have you done? What were the savings? Is it documented? Do you have some references to cite?

Customers Want to Reduce Operating Costs

Most organizations (even nonprofits) are trying to take costs out of doing what they do. If they're operating a manufacturing or distribution facility, they want to use less power. Contractors want to spend less on tools. So do hospitals and schools. You need to know enough about how your customers operate to be able to help them reduce these costs. What have you done recently to take costs out of a customer's operation? How much did it save that customer? Is it documented?

Customers Want to Reduce Health and Safety Costs

Some organizations are concerned about reducing health and safety costs. Such reductions often can result in lower insurance premiums or claims. (And think how much easier it is to recruit good people when you're not maiming them regularly as part of doing business.) Which of your current customers might have an initiative to reduce these costs? If they reduce their claims, what impact will it have on their cost of doing business? Do you have examples of companies reducing their insurance premiums by 15% when they implemented some of your recommendations?

Customers Want to Go Green

Many organizations are making an effort to go green. Doing so may provide a competitive advantage with their customers, save money, or simply give them a warm feeling about being good citizens. What products/services does your organization offer that would help your customers and prospects implement a green solution?

Customers Want to Retail Your Product

If you sell a product to organizations that resell it in a retail environment, you have another specific set of things the customer should consider. Your retail customers are interested in the inventory turns (as are other organizations), but more so. They're also interested in better ways to merchandise their products and in how much value they get from each square foot of display space. They should (but may not) understand the value of linking up product sales. You need to understand how your product helps customers who retail get more money out of your product.

Case Studies as a Sales Tool

For all of the customer goals listed above and others, your goal is to put together a few examples in which someone in your organization has been successful in helping a customer accomplish one of those goals. Put together a handful of case studies that include the following elements:

- a description of the customer
- a description of the application
- a discussion of what the customer was doing
- a presentation of your solution
- a cost-benefit statement.

The best way to present these cases, when possible, is to write them up and get the involved customers to type them on letterhead and sign them. Your most powerful sales presentations are made when current customers tell potential customers how good you are.

A Little Philosophy about Competitive Advantage

Before customers buy anything, they have to answer the following question: Do I believe that [*product/service name*], provided by [*company name*] and supported by [*salesperson's name*], meets my needs? The process may be formal and take months, or it may be informal and take 30 seconds, but it has to happen. Otherwise, you can't make the sale.

There are only three answers that customers can give to that question: "Yes." "No." "Maybe."

- **Yes.** The customer thinks you can do what needs to be done. The customer *can* buy from you—might not, but can.

- **No.** The customer decides that you can't do what needs to be done. The customer *cannot* buy from you—simple as that.

- **Maybe.** The customer is not sure that the product/your organization/you can do what needs to be done. The customer *will not* buy from you. (Because the customer already is getting what is needed from your competitor, remember?)

As you put together your value propositions, keep that customer question in mind. How will you prove the value of your product/service/company/self? How can you present your product so that the answer to that question is an unqualified "yes"?

Rings of Value

As you prepare your value propositions, begin by thinking about what you sell in terms of "rings of value" (exhibit 3-1). For everything that is sold, there are three different categories of value:

- the core product/service
- the value added by your company (and your vendors)
- the value added by you, the salesperson.

Product/Service: The Core Circle of Value

The product or service is at the center. The customer writes a purchase order (and a check) for the chemical supplies that you want to sell. ("Service" here refers to an activity you are selling, such as repairing a pizza oven; not to the service provided by your organization as part of the sale.) For every product or service that you sell, there are separate rings of value. You need to know what these values are for all of your focus products and services or product and service categories.

Exhibit 3-1. Rings of Value.

You also must understand how customers do their evaluations here. Some evaluations are very formal. For example, if you provide samples or give product demonstrations, you're giving the customer an opportunity to do a formal evaluation. Some customers may require that you be "on the drawing" before you are considered for a purchase. (Note that you can be on the drawing but not ever make a sale. However, if being on the drawing is part of the process, you have to know who is involved in this decision and how it works. I'll provide more detail on the customer's qualification process in chapter 6.) Other processes are much less formal. A customer might ask you who else uses or sells the product, and your answer may be all the product qualification the customer needs.

The following possible rings of value are discussed below: product quality, product performance, and product operating costs.

Product Quality. Saying that you sell a "quality" product means nothing. For "quality" to be a competitive advantage, the product that you're selling must have documented quality with a corresponding hard cost savings.

Here's an example: Competitive valves need to be replaced every three years. Your valve has a standard life of five years before replacement.

This would mean that the real cost of your valve is $x\%$ less than the competitive valve because of the longer use. Here's how the calculation would work: Your valve costs $800 and lasts five years. The competitive valve costs $600 and lasts three years. Because the competitive valve lasts only three years, the customer will have to purchase another valve to match the five-year life of your valve. So, the real cost of the competitive valve is $600 + $396 (that is, 0.66 x $600), or $986. By purchasing your valve, the customer can see hard cost savings of $196 (+ replacement/downtime costs—whatever time is lost to replace the valve) over the five-year life of your valve. The sales equation is

Real sales opportunity = Valve + $196 in savings
+ Replacement/downtime costs.

Product Performance. Stating that your product "outperforms" the competition is useless. If you say it, you need to be able to document what that means and demonstrate the real value.

Let's consider this example: Your cutting tool is diamond coated and very precise. In a particular application using your tool, only one of every 1,000 cuts has to be reworked or scrapped. The competitor's tool produces 2.2 reworked/scrapped parts in the same application. Your tool costs $48. The competitive tool costs $40. The rework/scrap cost to the customer is $22. By purchasing your cutting tool, the customer can see hard cost savings of $18.40. The calculation is this: your cutting tool costs $70—$48 + $22 (1 rework)—and the competitor's tool costs $88.40—$40.00 + $48.40 (2.2 reworks x $22). The sales equation is

Real sales opportunity = Cutting tool +
$18.40 savings in lower rework/scrap costs.

Product Operating Costs. Some products cost more to use than others—think maintenance, power, and changeover costs. Again, simply stating that it "costs less" to use your product than to use the current product is not helpful. You have to prove it. Maintenance costs refer to the amount of time spent keeping the product functioning at peak capacity. You possibly are looking at time or lubricant costs here. Power is simple: some products use more power than others use to deliver the same results. Changeover costs refer to the time required to switch from one application to another.

Here's an example focusing on lower maintenance costs: Your product needs to be cleaned and relubricated once in every 1,000 hours of usage. The estimated time to do that is 15 minutes. Local maintenance costs are $28 per hour. Your product costs $1,000. The competitor's product needs to be cleaned and relubricated every 500 hours, and the estimated time to do so is one hour (at the same rate). For discussion purposes, let's assume that the equipment runs 24 hours a day, all year. In a year, there are 8,760 hours, so your product would need to be lubricated 8.7 times. Total maintenance time required = 2.175 hours (8.7 lubrication events x 15 minutes). Total annual maintenance operating cost for your product is $60.90 (that is, 2.175 x $28). Your competitor's maintenance costs would be $490.56 (17.52 maintenance events x $28 per hour). This means that your product posts an annual maintenance savings of $429.66. Over the life of your product, this might make enough of a difference to get the customer to switch.

• • •

There also are lots of other areas where your product might be differentiated. Don't forget the value added by your vendors:

- a 24-hour technical hotline
- online support or technical information
- field visits from your vendors' field application engineers
- ability to custom-design some solutions.

All of these (and more) could end up being rings of value that differentiate what you sell from what the competition sells. None of these works, however, if you're trying to sell exactly the same product that a customer currently is using. Getting the customer to switch in that case normally results in a sale dependent on the cheapest price or availability. That may suggest you should look for areas where your solution differs from what the customer currently is using.

The Value Offered by Your Company

The second family of rings of value is the organization for which you work. For a lot of distributors, this is the first area where you really can differentiate from the competition. (We're all selling the same things these days.) So, your challenge is to know what your company does that is different from your competitors. Note that doing the same thing as your competitors is not really a ring of value. When I work with companies to help them determine their rings of value, I always put a list together and then go through it to determine what the organization does differently from its competitors. When "free local shipping" comes up, I always ask, "Are you the only ones who do that?" After a little mumbling, the answer often is that everyone offers it. So, that's not really a competitive advantage, right? It's just table stakes. The company has to do it to be in the game, but it doesn't help the company win.

As with products, there are both formal and informal reviews. A formal process would be getting your company on an approved vendor list. The informal process might be the question, Who else do you work with? Again, you need to understand who makes the evaluation and how it works.

When you're talking about the product/service rings of value, you often can come up with specific cost savings based on real data. When you move into the discussion of company rings of value, there are fewer hard data points, but you still have to demonstrate hard dollar savings—often in areas like labor productivity (downtime, throughput, call-backs). This means that you have to create a list of case studies that you can use with different customers.

Some possible areas for company advantages would be inventory, technical support, value added, and ease of doing business with you.

Inventory. We have it, they don't. To use this one, you have to know that it's true. Do you have any information from the customer base that says that Competitor X often is out of stock? If so, you may be able to use that information. But remember that you also have to put a hard value on everything that you present as a competitive advantage. For example, you believe that because of your inventory, your company can ship the same day on more than 99% of what your customer needs. But for every event where you can't get the product when needed, the cost to the customer is x dollars. You have to be able to calculate that cost.

Take, as an example, an electrical contractor who needs an item to complete a job. What's the cost of moving the crew from Job A to Job B, and then back to Job A when the product the crew needs finally arrives? What is the cost of travel time? What is the optimum time that a crew should work on a job? What are the costs of sending one guy back to a job to hook up a $9 part that your competitor did not have in stock? Furthermore, how often did the customer have these kinds of events on the last few jobs? (Never say anything bad about the competition. Just ask questions that move the prospect over to an area where you want to have a discussion.)

You can see that you really have to understand your customer's business to calculate the real value of your inventory investment. I'll make up a mythical example here. Let's say that the customer is smart enough to know that every hour of lost production costs $65 and that about 20 hours are lost each month as a result of out-of-stock situations from the distributors. The customer's annual cost of dealing with your competitors, therefore, would be the cost of what the customer buys + $15,600 (20 x 12 x $65). (Most customers probably would not know these numbers, so you need some industry data to support what you say, or you need to help the customer capture the data, if you plan to make this part of your company's competitive advantage.)

Understand that if you cannot link your inventory to positive financial benefits for your prospects or customers, they will be highly unlikely to change distributors.

Technical Support. Your company also may provide a high level of technical support. Application specialists within your company would be an example of this advantage. Proving the value of this element requires effort. You can't just state that your organization provides a high level of technical support.

Here's an example: When working with Customer A, one of your technical specialists helped the customer use a different product. The customer was able to shave 2.7 hours off of every HVAC installation. Because the customer normally uses a two-person crew, and the average cost per hour/per person is $17, the customer saved an average of $91.80 in labor on every installation. The calculation is 2.7 hours x 2 people x

$17 per hour. If you can connect this story to the prospect you're trying to sell now, you can create the perception of real value if the customer gives you an order.

Value Added. Much overused and misunderstood within distribution is the concept of "value-added services." Nothing is wrong with the concept; it's the presentation that bugs me. As a distribution salesperson, you can't just say things like, "We offer kitting, subassembly, and just-in-time delivery to the job site." There is no inherent value in that. Once again, you need to prepare some numbers to establish the value.

An example might look like this: When working with Customer B, we put together a complete job kit of everything the crew needed. The kit cost $120 more than the company was paying its current distributor for the materials, but the kit saved an average of 7 hours of labor on typical jobs. Because the company calculated hourly cost at $47, the average savings was $209 per job (7 hours x $47 = $329 – the additional $120 for the kitted product).

Ease of Doing Business. This value is important, but it is significantly more difficult to prove than are some of the other applications. Under ease of doing business, we might include the following elements:

- locations
- business hours
- local delivery
- credit policy
- knowledgeable counter salespeople.

All of those elements might be true, but remember that you're looking for areas where you do something that your competitors don't do. How many of your competitors state that they're located in inconvenient places, are only open for an hour a day, make the customer pick up everything, enforce tough credit policies, and have incompetents working the counter? All of that may be true, but your competitors probably don't advertise it. Even if your company has a real advantage here, the challenge is in demonstrating the value to the customer. Some advantages are easier to present than others.

Here's an example: If your branch is located within 30 minutes of most of your customers, and your competitors are trying to serve the same area from a facility an hour away, you (theoretically) should be able to save the customer 30 minutes of downtime when something is needed. The questions to be addressed are these: How often does the customer need that kind of service? How much do those 30 minutes cost the customer? If the customer doesn't know the answer to either question—and you can't get the customer to find out—your competitive advantage of being more convenient just goes up in smoke.

The Value of the Distribution Salesperson

The final set of value rings is provided by the salesperson. (That's you, in case you were wondering.) This is the toughest evaluation of all, but it's almost never formal. This evaluation underscores the old saying, "You only get one chance to make a good first impression." That's why things like showing up late, wearing rumpled clothes, and needing a shave are not likely to result in a big order for you.

There are things that customers look for in distribution salespeople, and these things can be rings of value that differentiate you from your competition. Some surveys show that the top two are

- follow-through skills
- problem-solving skills.

Strange that relationship and product knowledge didn't make the top of the list, isn't it? Negotiating skills and integrity also failed to make it to the top of the list.

As with the company rings of value, the salespeople rings of value need more anecdotal support (preferably with customer references) because you really must focus on adding value to the mix. As an example, let's take follow-though skills. The distribution salesperson might state the following: "From the time we get an opportunity until you get a quote, it takes an average of one day. For most of our customers, this means they can get their quotes to their customers three to five days faster. The real value here is that our customers say they increase their close percentages by a minimum of 5% after they start working with us. And here are testimonials from a couple of people you might know." That sales pro is demonstrating follow-through skills by showing that things don't lie around on the desk for a few days. The rep drives quotes through to completion. The benefit to the customer is that the rep's efforts help the customer win more business. The salesperson is hoping the prospect can do the math and come up with the value of winning 5% more quotes. If the sales rep has some data, the statement might look like this: "Most contractors of your size quote about $2 million a year. If you increase your hit ratio by 5%, that would be an additional $100,000 in sales without adding any cost to your business—just based on your distributor supplier being a little faster with answers."

PUTTING IT ALL TOGETHER

A sales pro for a chemical distributor was trying to get a new customer in the printing business. The prospect's current distributor had just been acquired by a large national firm and was becoming more "corporate." Because of this, the existing distributor had tightened up terms and was forcing the printer to take larger quantities of product to satisfy the minimums. The salesperson, knowing that his product was the same as his competitor's and that the printer had a good and long-standing relationship with the competing salesperson, decided that the only real rings of value would be provided by his company.

The sales pro met with the printer and did an evaluation of two things— the average amount of chemicals used on a monthly basis and the average total of the prospect's accounts receivable (A/R). He then went to his management and got them to agree to ship the customer the average monthly minimums and to allow the customer to pay on the basis of its average A/R days (which was 42 days).

The sales pro won the business because of the value proposition of product + more flexible supplier. The good news: the price was higher because the printer did not have to order in large quantities or pay within 30 days.

Conclusion

As you have been reading along here, I know what you've been thinking: I don't know any of my "rings of value." Great. Now you know what you need to learn to be more effective. Selling is not walking in, telling a few jokes, showing the purchasing agent a line card or catalog, and hoping that the agent gives you an opportunity to quote on something someday. Professional selling is understanding your customer's business, understanding the value of everything you sell (product/service, company, yourself), and matching up what you have with what customers need so that you can get them to do something different.

If you can't define the + *something else,* then you don't have a realistic chance of booking the order (unless you happen to be the consistently cheapest distributor in the marketplace). If that's not your value proposition, better spend some time developing a few new ones.

FOLLOW-UP ASSIGNMENTS

1. Select the focus products for which you intend to create a formal value proposition. Start with at least three of your focus products.

2. Do a formal assessment of your top three competitors for those products. Remember that your focus products may be replacing a different kind of product for a specific application. Don't forget all the rings of value your competitor offers.

3. Put together a defined value proposition for each of the focus products chosen. Make sure that you have something different to offer. Remember what customers really want:
    *   to sell more
    *   to increase price and improve margins
    *   to reduce inventories
    *   to reduce scrap, rework, and warranty costs
    *   to increase throughput and decrease downtime
    *   to reduce operating costs
    *   to reduce health and safety costs
    *   to go green.

Remember the sales equation: Real sales opportunity = Product/service + *Something else.*

4. Put together a short presentation, and remember to include a case study or two.

5. Look at your target account list, and select at least three places where you can sell one of your focus products.

The Overview of the Selling Process

Before you begin, answer these questions:

1. Selling can be divided into two sets of questions—those the customer needs to answer and those the salesperson needs to answer. In sequence, what questions does the customer need to answer before deciding to buy?
2. In sequence, what questions does the salesperson need to answer to get an order?

The debate has raged for many years: is selling an art or a science? In my humble opinion, it's both. The bad news is that if you were not born with the "artistic" talent of sales, no one can teach it to you. The art side is all about charisma and likability. The good news is that by learning the "science" or process side of selling, you can become one of the top professionals in the world and earn a nice living.

This chapter is an introduction to the process of selling. You're going to get two different looks at it—the macro (big-picture) view and the micro (step-by-step) view. In each of these views, you will learn how to determine both where you are and what you need to do to maximize your effectiveness.

The Big Picture

Exhibit 4-1 is designed to give you a quick understanding of what happens in the distribution sales process, predominantly from the customer's point of view. No matter what you're selling, customers go through this process. In some cases, the process is very formal, takes

Exhibit 4-1. TAC versus PUC.

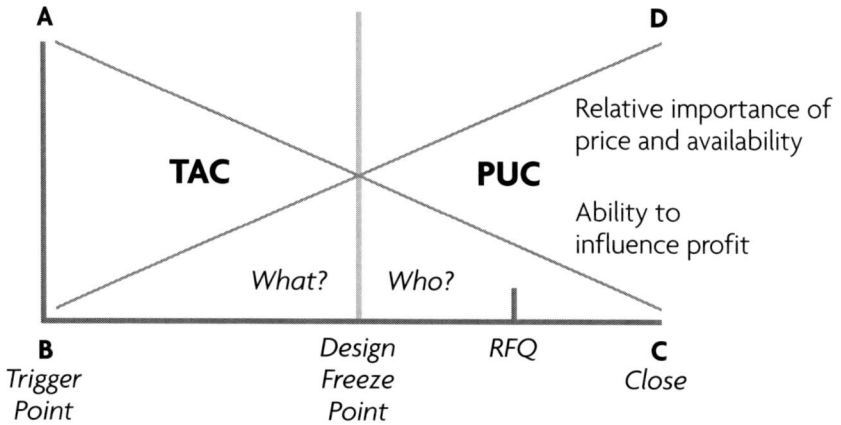

A · D

TAC · · · · · · · · · · · · · · **PUC**

Relative importance of price and availability

Ability to influence profit

What? · · · *Who?*

B · · · · · · · · · · · · · · · *Design* · · · *RFQ* · · · C
Trigger · · · · · · · · · · · *Freeze* · · · · · · · · · *Close*
Point · · · · · · · · · · · · *Point*

months, and involves dozens of people. Other times, one person does it very informally in a matter of minutes. Either way, these things have to happen, and you need to know the answers to a few questions:

- What is the process?
- Who is involved?
- What is the timing?

This process also defines one of the most important issues in selling: how important price (and delivery) will be to the customer, and how much time/effort you probably will have to spend dealing with the dreaded price objection.

Let's begin by understanding exhibit 4-1. The chart contains five lines and four points. The first vertical line (A–B) is the *importance line.* The higher you go on this line, the more important something is.

The horizontal line (B–C) is the *time line,* which represents the time line of each individual sale. Each opportunity has its own life—it's born, it grows, it lives, and it dies. (Note that you might have five different opportunities at five different points along this line with the same customer.)

The second vertical line is the *design freeze line.* This line represents the point in the sale when customers know what they want.

The diagonal lines represent the two key arguments that go on in every customer's decision-making process. The line from A to C is the *value line*. Customers always want value—even if they are talking about price. No one wants to buy a pair of shoes for $1 and have those shoes fall apart the first time they're worn. This line also represents two important things for the distribution salesperson: the ability to influence the outcome of the sale and the likelihood of a profitable sale.

The line from B to D is the *price line*. This line represents the importance of price and availability in the customer's decision-making process.

There also are four points along the B–C line. The first point is the *trigger*. This is where customers decide that they need (or want) something. The second point is the *design freeze point*. The third point is the *request for quote* (RFQ) point, and the final point (*close*) is at position C. (If you want to think of a name for D, just think "defeated" because that's what happens when price and availability assume that level of importance in the sale.)

So far, here's what we have: A sale begins at the trigger point and moves along a time line until the customer decides from whom to purchase. This decision can take less than a minute, or it can take months, depending on the circumstances. Your ability to influence the sale (and the profitability) can be very high if you get involved at or near the trigger, or it can be very low if you get involved at the RFQ. The importance of price and availability can be either very low (at or near the trigger) or very high (if you get involved at the RFQ). Take your finger or a marker of some sort and make a few marks along the B–C line (yes, it's okay to write in the book). Then make marks directly above those points on both the A–C and the B–D line. This should help you understand the concept. The proverbial bottom line on the chart is that the later you get involved, the harder it is to make the sale, unless you have better availability, the best price, or both.

The Trigger Point (Bang!)

The trigger point is where customers decide they need or want something. The best possible selling is when the salesperson is there at that moment. Here's a scenario: The customer is using belting in its conveying process. The belt breaks. The customer knows what is needed to replace it. If you're not there, the customer probably will decide to replace it with exactly the same belting that's currently being used—and will buy it from the same source as last time. But if you were there when the belt broke, you might be able to convince the customer not to buy belting that breaks but to buy a better belt from you.

Another example might be a little more complicated: A customer has a quality problem. A decision is made to reengineer the line. The line uses belting. If you're not involved in this process of redesigning the line, the customer may specify a competitor's belting—without you ever having had a chance to quote it. But if you are involved in the process, you might be able to get your belting specced . . . and the customer might buy it from you . . . and you might *not* have to be the cheapest.

The Design Freeze Point (It's Very Cold on the Right Side of the Design Freeze Point)

If you're a perceptive person (and because you're reading this book, I have to assume you are), you may have noticed that the design freeze point occurs exactly where the lines A–C and B–D intersect. For the distribution salesperson, chances of getting the order at good margins are best at the top of the A–C line, and they diminish as the line heads toward the C point. Conversely, the importance of price and availability in the customer's decision-making process increases with the upward slope of the B–D line. Where the lines intersect also breaks the sale into two distinct halves: TAC and PUC. We will discuss these next, but you need to understand that the design freeze point is the point in the process where the customer says, "This is what I need." When you are on the left side of that point, your ability to influence the sale is greater than the importance of price/availability. When that line is crossed, your ability to influence declines, relative to price and availability.

TAC. The left half of the sales process is labeled "TAC" (total acquisition cost). Pronounced "tack." This is the portion of the process where the customer answers the question, What do I need? The process can be formal and involve many people, or it can be informal, with one person making the decision. You not only need to understand this process, but you also need to be involved in it as often as possible.

There are many factors that make up a customer's TAC. Ideally, your value proposition will line up with what the customer is trying to accomplish. Listed here are some of the factors that make up the customer's TAC:

- cost of generating a quote
- cost of generating a purchase order
- cost of inventory
- cost of quality
- cost of throughput
- cost of downtime
- cost of internal handling
- cost of packaging
- cost of scrap/rework
- cost of call-backs or warranties
- cost of time
- cost of lost opportunities
- cost of money
- cost of accidents (health/safety)
- cost of power
- cost of maintenance
- cost of disposal (environmental costs).

To sell effectively, you want to get the customer to understand the "total" cost of purchasing an item. Here are a few examples:

- **Cost of inventory**—The competitor's product costs $100, but the customer has to buy a minimum of $5,000 (50 parts) to get that price. Your product costs $110, but you will sell the customer *one* if that's all that is needed. Unless the customer uses 50 at a time, your TAC is cheaper than your competitor's because the customer doesn't have to order 50 at a time.

- **Cost of call-backs**—The competitor's product costs $40. The customer ends up doing 10–15 call-backs per year because the competitor's product fails. Your product costs $50, but it prompts only about 10% of the competitor's call-backs (1–2 per year). In this case, your product has a cheaper TAC because those additional 9–14 annual call-backs cost the customer a lot of money.

- **Cost of lost opportunities**—The competitor's products cost $100 and yours cost $150. The customer needs quick answers so that bids go out on time. Orders are lost when bids are late. The customer loses five to six jobs a month because information from your competitor isn't received on time. Your product might be a lot "cheaper" (based on lost sales) if you can guarantee the customer a same-day answer on quotes and the customer is able to win more jobs.

This is why the best distribution salespeople try to do most of their selling between the trigger point and the design freeze point. When they're selling here, they have the greatest chance to win business—without being the cheapest—because they help answer the customer's question, What do I need?

This is also why TAC has the subtitle "What?" From the moment when customers know they need something, they work to answer the question, What? If you help them answer this question, you're more likely to win business at good margins. If they answer without you (perhaps in discussions with your competitor), you'll have a much harder time winning, and the issue will often boil down to these two questions:

- Who has it? (availability)
- What does it cost? (price)

If prospects have never bought from you before, Sir Isaac reminds us that they probably won't buy from you this time either.

PUC. The right half of the sales process is labeled "PUC" (per-unit cost—pronounced "puke"). In the TAC section, I listed a lot of the elements that make up the customer's total acquisition cost. I'll do the same for PUC. Are you ready? Here goes:

- the price of the product
- the availability of the product.

Do you hear the crickets? That's all there is to this portion of the sales process. When you cross the line, you end up in the worst kind of sale discussion. The customer tells you what is needed, asks if you have it, asks your price—and then probably buys it from your competitor anyway if it was bought from that source before. Your quote only served as a price-check—or if you got aggressive, the customer used your low number to bludgeon your competitor into a price concession . . . but that competitor still got the order.

The only exception to this would be if having items in stock is your company's value proposition. If you have immediate availability and your competitors do not, then you can win business here, without having to be the cheapest. If that's your company's value proposition, you're in good shape. If not, ...

The PUC side of the chart is subtitled "Who?" After the customer has decided "what" is needed, a question must be answered: From whom are we going to buy it? The vast majority of customers will buy "it" from the same distributor—especially if the "what" is the same as last time.

The Bottom Line

Professional salespeople work to create a different "what" so that they have a greater chance to be the "who" getting the order.

Here's an example: A plumbing contractor has been buying a certain brand of fittings for years. An astute salesperson calls on the contractor and tells the prospect about "quick-connect" fittings that allow the contractor to install more hardware in less time. This enables the contractor to do the following:

- Bid jobs a little lower (less labor) and possibly win more work.

- Do more jobs with the same crew in the same time (more profit).

- Hire cheaper people because the quick-connect fittings don't require the same skill set as the old fittings required (bigger labor pool, more profits).

Go back to the value proposition and our definition of a real opportunity, and you get the following equation:

Real opportunity = Fittings + (Lower-cost jobs + More jobs in same time + Cheaper labor for the contractor)

In this case, the salesperson redefined "what" the customer needed and got an opportunity to win the business—without necessarily being the cheapest.

The Micro View

The first look that we took at the sales process was primarily a customer view. The second look is more micro—and is really focused on the distribution salesperson's view of the sales process. (This specifically is *not* the process for a professional sales call. The distributor sales call will be covered later, but this portion of the discussion is about the process of

---

PUTTING IT ALL TOGETHER

For more than a year, an electrical distribution salesperson had been trying to sell wire, connectors, and terminal blocks to a prospect. He regularly met with purchasing and got opportunities to quote on the items that he wanted to sell. Over the course of a year, he had quoted more than 20 pieces of business, but never won any of them. The purchasing person told him that his prices were "too high"—when he got any explanation at all.

On one occasion, however, one of the engineers at the company had called him to ask a question about a specific application. (The engineer did not know from whom the company was buying and randomly had picked an electrical distributor out of the phone book to get his question answered.) This was a product that had never been discussed with the salesperson, so he scheduled an appointment with the engineer to provide the answer.

During the appointment, the salesperson learned that the company was developing a new product. He was able to work with the engineer to establish his product specifications as part of the bill of materials. He also found out that the engineering staff had a technical purchasing support person who bought products used in new designs. This person was not in the purchasing department, but was part of product engineering.

The salesperson not only won the order (at good margins), but also had the opportunity to be involved in future discussions with the engineers as they redesigned various products to take costs out.

This is a classic example of getting involved in the TAC portion of the process and helping the customer define "what" is needed.

---

selling something.) In later chapters, we are going to take a much more detailed look at each of the steps of the process, but you need an overview so that you can fit everything in context.

A Few Simple Principles

I hope you agree that selling has some process steps. Before going into the process itself, there are a few concepts that you need to consider.

First, each step must be completed. There are six steps in the sales process. Each step is really a mini-sale. You have to get six very specific "yes" answers—one at the end of each step of the process. Think of the process as a road to success. At the end of each step of the process, there is an intersection. At each intersection, you'll see a traffic signal. The signal tells you whether to continue or stop. When you drive along a road, you can't skip a section of road unless you take a detour. Just like driving, a detour in sales can lead you away from the path you want to follow and may use a lot more time and energy than necessary. Don't be in a hurry to get to the next step. Do each step properly and completely, and you'll see an increase in sales (and a decrease in the amount of work required to make your budget).

Second, each of the six specific steps must be done in sequence. You wouldn't send someone a quote and *then* find out what that person wanted. Many distribution salespeople are in a hurry to get through the sale, so they skip steps. When you skip a step, one of the following things usually happens:

- You get a "no."

- You have to go back and do the things that you missed, thus making the process longer and harder.

- You go back and do things that you missed, and then get a "no" anyway—the worst result of all.

Third, you must get "yes"/"no" answers. The traffic light analogy is a good one because it should get you thinking about what happens at traffic lights. They have three colors: green, yellow (amber, if you prefer), and red. These colors are symbolic of the three major answers that you get in sales:

- green = yes
- yellow = maybe
- red = no.

So, when you get to the end of each part of the sales process, you need to ask yourself, What color is the light? If it's green, go on to the next step. If it's red, stop. But what should you do if it's yellow? The strong recommendation is to understand that most "maybe" answers in sales really mean "no." If you can get that understood, selling becomes a lot easier because you'll begin to recognize the fluffy answers or lack of answers as a lack of interest in doing business with you. Then you can make an informed decision either to identify what the objection is or to move on so that you do not waste time on an opportunity that you have no reasonable expectation of booking.

One little warning about the steps: Each step may not represent a sales call. You can go from the beginning to the end of an opportunity in one sales call lasting six minutes. You have made such calls. The customer currently uses your product; another one is needed; you are asked if you have it and what it costs; you give the customer the information; and the customer gives you the purchase order. One call, six minutes or less.

You also can make multiple sales calls in each step of the sale. You might make three calls on the customer simply to find the right person to approach. Remember that the steps do not represent sales calls; they represent the specific elements of a sale that must be done every time, in the prescribed order, for you ultimately to make a sale.

And Now the Steps

Exhibit 4-2 presents the sales pipeline, a graphic way to illustrate the six steps of the sales process. In the following sections, I'll tell you about the steps; and in later chapters, I'll go into greater detail about each step.

Step 1: Identify/Qualify the Customer. This is the first thing that you have to do to sell something to a customer. For prospects, this takes longer and might involve Internet research and maybe even a site visit before you decide that you actually can (or even should) sell the customer something.

Exhibit 4-2. The Sales Pipeline.

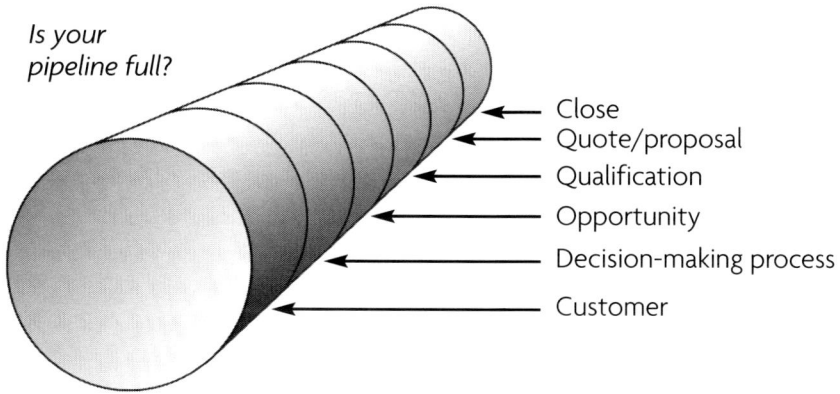

Is your pipeline full?

← Close
← Quote/proposal
← Qualification
← Opportunity
← Decision-making process
← Customer

At this step, you are trying to answer two questions:

1. How much potential exists?
2. Can the customer pay the bills?

How much potential exists? Before spending a lot of time on a prospect, you need to have some idea of how much the prospect can buy from you over a year. What is your estimate of the possible purchaser's potential? For existing customers, you should have a good feel for this; for prospects, it's more difficult. You also need some understanding of the value of your time. Answer the following question for your territory: For a customer that currently buys $50,000 a year and has the potential to buy another $50,000 a year, how much time should I spend? If you have a clear answer (perhaps, 10 field calls and a monthly phone call), then you're in good shape. (Those may not be the right numbers for your business, but you get the point. You need to have some understanding of how much time you must spend with an account.) If you don't have a clear answer, the odds are that you're spending too much time with some accounts and not enough time with others. To answer the questions, you need to know customer/prospect potential and to have some rule of thumb that drives the way you spend your time.

Can they pay their bills? No sale is complete unless we get paid. If you get a purchase order, will your credit department let you ship it? Will the buyer pay? You need to address this question early in the process. Using the traffic light analogy, what would happen if you booked an order with an account that might not be able to pay its bills? You would get a yellow light at the first intersection, followed by a string of green lights—right up to the end, when you get a red light. If you're going to get a red light, you want to get it as early as possible, and where it really occurs—not at the end of the process, after you have invested a lot of time.

This step should take little time with an existing customer: you just need to confirm that the customer is still creditworthy. But on new accounts and prospects, this is a step where you need to spend some additional time.

Step 2: Identify/Qualify the Decision-Making Process. When you know that you are dealing with a qualified customer (one with enough potential for you to care), the next step is to understand the decision-making process (DMP). Here again, you are answering two critical questions:

1. Who is involved?
2. How does it work?

Who is involved? The first question seeks to understand who actually makes decisions. This question is very difficult because the "right" answer changes:

- Different job titles make different kinds of decisions at different organizations. You have seen this in practice. At one company, engineering makes all the decisions about new products; at another, purchasing makes the decisions.

- Different products sometimes have different decision makers. You may be selling Product A to Bill. You assume that Bill is the decision maker for Product B. Bill may have some say, but the truth is that Mary is really the final decision maker on Product B. If you leave Mary out and try to work it through Bill, it will take longer than it should, and the result probably will not be what you want it to be.

- Sometimes, decision making changes from time to time without apparent reasons. Organizations often go through changes that are not always obvious to an outsider. So, although Bill may have been the decision maker, the customer's decision to hire Fred and fire Jane may have created a completely new purchasing dynamic for the product you're trying to sell.

This is tricky because you really can't come out and ask Bill or Mary or Fred or Jane which of them is the decision maker. In the first place, it's kind of insulting; and in the second place, most people won't admit to *not* being important.

One other factor that you have to keep in mind is that, in many organizations, a decision to purchase something the organization has not purchased before (or something it has purchased but from a different distributor) has a different approval process. In cases like this, there is often an unwritten rule that at least two people need to be involved if there is anything different. Remember that a lot of people have the authority to buy what they bought before from the distributor they bought it from—but they do not have the authority to buy something new or even something old from someone new. Keep all of this in mind as you try to identify the "who."

How does it work? This is the better question. The goal of the distribution sales professional is to move the question from the "who" to the "how." Get customers to describe the process they use for selecting a new product or for using a new distributor, and you will enable the people you're talking with to give you better answers. Because you need to know how it works anyway, you sometimes can get all the information you need with this one simple question.

Step 3: Identify/Qualify the Opportunity. This is the step where it feels like you're doing some real "selling." The goal at this part of the process is to find a piece of business to work on. A lot of salespeople are way too passive here. The assumption is that the customer knows what the salesperson sells and will let the salesperson look at the opportunities that are relevant. This is often not the case, and distribution salespeople who think this way really are more "order takers" than salespeople.

A salesperson always should remember that little piece of philosophy presented in the first chapter:

Real sales power = Opportunities in excess of need.

To have consistent sales, you need to put a consistent amount of new opportunities into the pipeline. You also need to know/remember your historic close ratio. If you close 50% and your goal is to sell $50,000 per month, then you have to identify a minimum of $100,000 a month in *new* opportunities and put them into your pipeline. (To give yourself some real power, better make that a little more than $100,000.)

The question you're working on here looks like this: Is there a piece of business that the customer is willing to work on with me?

There are many pieces of business that meet the first part of the question, but not the second. As an example, you might identify a cost savings on a $5 part that is used once on a $200,000 bill of materials. This might seem like a big deal to you (you want to make a sale), but how important do you think that would be to the person in charge of the bill of materials? That item probably would not make that person's top 10 list for a long time.

Step 4: Identify/Qualify the Customer's Qualification Process. After you have found a piece of business (at a qualified customer, with the right decision maker[s]), the next step is getting that piece of business qualified by the customer. The customer has to answer this question: Do I believe that the solution offered by [*your name*] at [*your company's name*] meets my needs?

There are three possible answers to that question:

- **Yes.** A "yes" answer means that the customer *can* buy your product/service. This does not mean that the customer *will* do so, but that the customer is able to do so because your product or service meets the defined needs.

- **No.** A "no" answer means that the customer cannot buy your product/service.

- **Maybe.** A "maybe/I'm not sure" answer means that the customer probably will not buy your product. This is especially true if the customer already is purchasing some kind of solution that meets identified needs.

You also should note that the qualifying question has three parts:

- **Product/service.** This is the part of the qualification process with which we're most comfortable. Things like samples, testing, demos, and technical literature address this part of the question.

- **Company.** The customer buys not only a product but also a relationship with the organization that supplies it. Things like dependability, free shipping, and warranties enter into this.

- **You.** The final part of the question deals with the hardest part of the evaluation. The customer looks at you as part of the value being purchased (or not). This explains the historic emphasis on the "likability" of salespeople. If customers like you, they are more likely to buy from you. In today's world, there are other reasons, such as dependability and technical problem solving, that also are part of the equation.

As a professional, you need to understand who is involved and how it works. Again, in some organizations, this is a formal process that might involve being on an approved vendor list and undergoing facility audits. In other cases, it might take 30 seconds. Your job is to know as much about how it works as possible before you get there so that you can put your value into terms that are prized by the person/organization doing the evaluation.

Step 5: Present Quotes and Proposals. After you have completed the first four steps of the process, you are ready to provide the prospect with a quote. (I wonder how many quotes you have out there right now for which some portion of steps 1–4 has not been completed.)

The question that the customer is trying to answer is, What are they (really) offering? The customer wants to know what the price/availability is; and the customer may be interested in hearing about other items, such as terms and warranty information. This step is one of the most concrete parts of the sales process—at the end of the step, you either have presented the customer a quote or you haven't. For that reason, a lot of distribution salespeople are in such a big hurry to get here that they start the process by asking for permission to quote on something.

You need to remember that the quote should be a confirmation of your understanding of the customer's needs. If you're using the quote as a door-opener, then you have a different scenario where your quote really isn't real—it's just an opportunity for further discussion. In a real sales situation, the quote comes after the first four steps have been completed, not before.

A proposal differs slightly from a quote in that it is also educational. Remember the three things that the customer qualifies: product/service, organization, and salesperson. A proposal might have additional information about all three of these items. Normally, a proposal is used in more formal selling situations—especially those with multiple influencers and multiple competitors. Here's the best way to think about this: a quote is a "confirming" document, and a proposal is a "selling" document. When you use a proposal, you're acknowledging that you have some more selling to do—even though you're giving the customer all the information needed to make a buying decision.

Step 6: Close the Sale. The final step in the process is the close. You have not completed the process until you have asked the customer for the order. The customer's question here is, Am I going to buy this product/service from [*your name*] at [*your company's name*] here?

If you have done your job correctly, the customer will do a lot of the closing for you. Your job is to give the customer an opportunity to give you a "yes" or "no" answer. If you take the customer through this process—and finish with a scheduled close—you've done everything that a professional is asked to do.

Conclusion

As you have gone through the first few chapters, you probably have noticed the great emphasis on "process." Thinking about selling as a process, rather than strictly as an art form, should be comforting to you because you can begin to see the different steps—and that should drive you to think about selling as a sequential process rather than as a "black box" where you do something at the front end and hope that sales magically trickle out the other end.

As you read the descriptions, you probably could come up with some examples from your own experience where the sale followed the process, exactly as described. In other cases, you might not have been able to see the steps. This is because of the variability of people. Not all sales will follow the processes exactly—but enough of them will for you to use them as a guide. When in doubt, go back to the process. Try to determine where you are and what needs to be done to move the sale forward.

FOLLOW-UP ASSIGNMENTS

1. Compare the answers you gave to the questions at the beginning of the chapter with what you learned here. Compare what you said needs to happen—and the sequence—with the information presented in the chapter.

2. Review your list of open sales opportunities, and try to determine which opportunities were started in TAC versus PUC. Answer these questions:
   - What percent of your open opportunities are TAC?
   - What percent are PUC?

3. For three of the opportunities that were created in TAC (I hope you have at least that many), answer the following questions:
   - What kind of organization is it (market, size, ownership, and so forth)?
   - Which part of the organization did you start with (engineering, maintenance, purchasing, and the like)?
   - What was your value proposition?

4. Review your list of open sales opportunities again. Determine which step of the sales process (steps 1–6) you're in for each opportunity:
   - identify/qualify the customer
   - identify/qualify the decision-making process
   - identify/qualify an opportunity
   - identify/qualify the customer's qualification process
   - present quotes and proposals
   - close the sale.

5. Review your list to see if there are any gaps. Answer these questions:
   - Do you have any opportunities in steps 1 and 2?

- How much business is in step 3?
- Do you have anything in step 4?
- Are the bulk of your opportunities in step 5?
- Do you have any activity scheduled in step 6?

Prospecting—A Gold Mine, if You Dig It

Before you begin, answer these questions:

1. How much business did you get from new customers last year?
2. What is your prospecting goal?
3. How much business needs to come from new customers this year? From existing customers this year?
4. In the last month, how many hours did you spend either calling on new customers or calling on new people within existing customers?
5. In the last month, how many new-customer calls did you make? How many of those customers are good enough to warrant your making regular calls on them?
6. In the last month, how many new people did you identify at existing customers?
7. How many of those new customers are qualified financially?
8. What is the potential for the new business that you uncovered in the last month??

In this chapter and the next two, we're going to be discussing the six steps of the distributor sales process in more detail. The first two steps in the process involve the customer's organization and decision-making process. These two steps, when taken together, have another name: *prospecting.*

Prospecting for new customers and new people is one of the hardest parts of the distribution sales process. Most salespeople dislike it—with good reason. The payback is small, and the rejection is large. However, successful distribution salespeople are prospecting all the time.

To be effective, you need to start with an understanding of why it's so tough. Remember that every prospect already is buying what is needed from someone—and those purchases start by not wanting to change. The easiest decision for the customer is always to buy what always has been bought from the salesperson/distributor who always has supplied it. (Once again, your greatest enemy is not your competitor; it's Sir Isaac.) There are some rare times when you walk in, and the buyer is willing to see you. This is normally because the existing distributors have failed to deliver in one way or another. But most of the time, you'll be prospecting on people who are "happy" with their current distributors. Your job is to make them "unhappy," without making them feel bad in the process (or running down their current distributors).

You need to refer to the earlier discussion of the value proposition (chapter 3) and come up with some things you can offer potential buyers that they are not getting currently and that they will value enough to go through the grief of switching distributors.

You also need to remember that a decision to switch distributors has an element of risk for your prospects. If they decide to switch distributors, and you fail, they look really bad. You need to keep this in mind throughout the selling process and do everything you can to reduce or eliminate their risk.

The first two steps of the sales process are

1. identify/qualify the customer
2. identify/qualify the DMP.

When you step back, it makes sense—you have to find some new customers and then you have to find the right people inside those organizations to whom you can sell something. (You also have to find new people inside your existing accounts to whom you can sell different things—another form of prospecting.)

As a distribution sales pro, you begin every year with a goal of how much business you intend to get from new customers and the growth you want from your existing customers (which just might require that you find some new people inside existing accounts). You also want to get an understanding of how to budget your time.

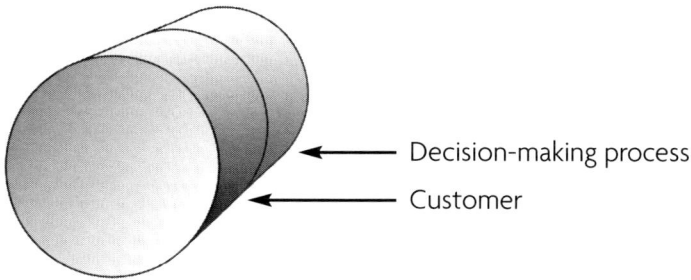

Decision-making process
Customer

Your Prospecting Goal

The first question that you have to answer is this: How much new business do I need? To answer this question, you have to know the following things:

- **Your sales goal**—What is your target for next year? Start with an understanding of what you're trying to accomplish—grow your territory by 5%, 10%, or 15%? You have to start with a number.

- **Your previous year's sales**—How much did you sell last year? You might not know the exact number, because you're probably doing your budgeting before the year ends, but you need to guesstimate your final sales so that you can determine the delta.

- **Your retention rate**—Year over year, how much business do you normally keep? This is tough to figure, and most salespeople don't have an answer. Look at how much business your existing customers do year over year before you add in the new sales. If you're looking for a rule of thumb (in a normal year), assume that you are losing between 10% and 15%. This means that you start in a hole, relative to the previous year's sales.

- **Customer share**—You know what you sold. What you need to figure out is how much you realistically can sell to your existing accounts. If you sold $1 million last year, is there another million in there, or another $250,000 that you actually could get, either by selling more of what you are already selling or by selling more products to the account?

- **Your diversification goal**—Over the next year, how do you
  want to change your territory to make it healthier? You might be
  able to get all the sales growth you need in your existing accounts, but should you? Do you want to add some different
  market niches to make your territory a little more recession
  proof next year? Do you have too many eggs in one basket? Do
  you need to lessen your reliance on a handful of customers by
  broadening your base? How much of that do you want to do
  next year?

- **Your focus products goal**—Do you need to find new customers
  to whom you can sell the focus products of your organization—
  or can you get that business from your existing customers? The
  final question that you need to address is one that determines
  where you go to get your focus product sales. There probably
  are some vendors that you need to support a little better than
  you did in the past year, right? There may be some new products that management wants you to push. There may be some
  margin improvement you need to make on some accounts by
  selling them items with higher margins. How much of that do
  you need to do next year?

By answering these questions, you can come up with a pretty clear plan
for how much prospecting you need to do. Exhibit 5-1 provides an example of a prospecting worksheet, and exhibit 5-2 is a blank worksheet
for you to complete. After you have filled it out, you will be able to complete the 3 x 3 sales matrix, which is your guide to how you need to
spend your prime sales time (7 a.m.–5 p.m.) during the year.

The 3 x 3 Sales Matrix, Again

Now would be a good time for you to dust off the 3 x 3 sales matrix from
chapter 2 because it will remind you of what you need to do (exhibit 5-3).

For the example presented in exhibit 5-3, the salesperson has a goal of
$1 million in total sales for the year. Look at the amount of sales budgeted
for boxes 3 and 4. Add these amounts together and divide the total by the
total sales goal to find the absolute minimum percentage of time that this
salesperson needs to spend working on prospecting for new accounts:

$$\text{Box 3 (100,000)} + \text{Box 4 (50,000)} = 150{,}000$$

$$150{,}000 \div 1{,}000{,}000 = 15\%$$

$$15\% \times 50 \text{ prime selling hours} = 7.5 \text{ hours per week.}$$

Do the same thing for box 2 to get some feel for the time the sales rep might need to spend finding new people inside existing accounts:

$$\text{Box 2} = 100{,}000$$

$$100{,}000 \div 1{,}000{,}000 = 10\%$$

$$10\% \times 50 \text{ prime selling hours} = 5 \text{ hours per week.}$$

In this scenario, the distribution salesperson would need to spend about 12.5 hours per week looking for new accounts and/or new people.

Step 1: Identify/Qualify the Customer

What Does Your "Them" Look Like?

Okay, you know what you need (and you've made a commitment to put a specific amount of effort into getting it). Now you need to create a picture of what "them" looks like. The best way to do this is to start with what you already have. For this exercise, you need to review your existing good customers and develop a profile of success.

Thinking of your best current customers, answer these questions: What types of organizations are they? Businesses? Nonprofits? Original equipment manufacturers? Maintenance and repair operations? If you're selling to retail customers, which ones are best for you? Big-box retailers? National chains? Local chains? Mom-and-pops? Are you doing well with new-install contractors or with maintenance/repair contractors? Are machine shops a good place for you to sell, or are hospitals better?

You're looking for trends here because if you have been successful with a certain type of organization, the easiest way to prospect is to find other businesses like that one. Not only do you know how to sell to them, but you also have instant credibility with new prospects because of your work with organizations with which they probably are familiar.

What else do you know about your good customers? Look at some of the other factors that might help you sell more effectively. Are your best

Exhibit 5-1. Prospecting Worksheet Example.

What were your sales for last year? What percentage of your customers' potential did you sell to them? What percentage came from your focus customers? What percent came from your focus products? How much existing business do you expect to lose this year? (The average is 10%–15%. What is reality for your territory?) Begin by establishing the baseline of what you have done.

> ### *Example:*
> Previous year's sales: $900,000
>
> Estimate of customer share: 20% *[This means there is an estimated additional $3,600,000 of potential sales within your existing customer base. That's enough to hit your distributor sales goal if no diversification is needed—and if the additional sales opportunities are for your focus products.]*
> - 50% to target customers
> - 40% from focus products
>
> Expected loss: $100,000
>
> Estimated base sales: $900,000 – $100,000 = $800,000
>
> Of that $800,000 in sales, you expect about 50% ($400,000) will be to focus customers and 40% ($320,000) will be focus products.

What is your sales goal for the year? How much new business do you need to accomplish your goal? What amount could come from your existing customers? What amount should come from that source? What amount should come from diversification?

> ### *Example:*
> Sales goal: $1,000,000
> - 60% to target customers ($600,000)
> - 50% from focus products ($500,000)
>
> Diversification goal: 10% [a subjective number used only for purposes of illustration]: $100,000

Deal with the "deltas."

> Total new sales needed: $1,000,000 versus $800,000 = $200,000
>
> New sales to focus customers needed: $600,000 versus $400,000 = $200,000
>
> New sales of focus products needed: $500,000 versus $320,000 = $180,000
>
> Sales needed to diversify territory: $100,000

These are the areas where your prospecting efforts need to be focused.

Exhibit 5-2. Prospecting Worksheet.

What were your sales for last year? What percentage of your customers' potential did you sell to them? What percentage came from your focus customers? What percentage came from your focus products? How much existing business do you expect to lose this year? (The average is 10%–15%. What is reality for your territory?) Begin by establishing the baseline of what you have done.

Example:

Previous year's sales: $ _____

Estimate of customer share: _____ %

- _____ % to target customers
- _____ % from focus products

Expected loss: $ _____

Estimated base sales: $ _____

_____ % to focus customers ($ _____)

_____ % from focus products ($ _____)

What is your sales goal for the year? How much new business do you need to accomplish your goal? What amount could come from your existing customers? What amount should come from that source? What amount should come from diversification?

Example:

Sales goal: $ _____

- _____ % to target customers ($ _____)
- _____ % from focus products ($ _____)

Diversification goal: _____ %: $ _____

Deal with the "deltas."

Total new sales needed: $ _____

New sales to focus customers needed: $ _____

New sales of focus products needed: $ _____

Sales needed to diversify territory: $ _____

Exhibit 5-3. The 3 x 3 Sales Matrix.

Raise Prices	Existing Products	New Products
Existing Customers	1 750,000	2 100000
New Customers	3 100,000	4 50,000

customers locally owned/managed? Do they do less than $25 million in sales? Do they have more than 100 employees? Are they strong engineering-driven companies or purchasing-driven organizations? Is decision making centralized or decentralized? It's important that you see what your current good customers have in common. Regardless of what you now are selling to them, could you sell them more than $100,000 or less than $25,000? What can your sales to good customers teach you about the available potential at other customers and prospects?

The profile you create by answering those questions will help you target similar customers, but what about different customers? In some of the previous questions, you were challenged to think about two questions that might just drive you out of your comfort zone: How much effort should you put into diversifying your customer base? How much effort do you need to put into selling more focus products?

1. **What is your diversification goal?** Maybe your current accounts are good, long-term customers. Maybe not. Are you concerned that some of your customers might be a little shaky? Do you need to add some different kinds of customers to make your territory healthier? What do those customers look like? Do you need to add some government customers to balance out your heavy business portfolio? Do you need to find some customers who work in the winter to balance out your existing customers' tendency to grow pretty dormant from January to April? Create a picture of the new business that you want. This will come in

really handy when you're putting together a list to target. If you simply are going after "new business," everyone looks the same. Use your prospecting efforts to build a healthier territory.

2. **What is your focus products goal?** You probably have some vendors that you need to support. You also probably have some products/services that have higher margins—perhaps some pay a higher commission. Start with a list of the products/services that you need to focus on over the coming year. Where can you sell them? The easiest place to sell them probably is in your portfolio of existing customers, but is that the best place? To sell some focus products, do you need to target some different types of customers? Which types of organizations are more likely to buy the products that you *want* to sell?

Where Can You Find Them?

By this point, you have put together a pretty good description of the kinds of new customers that you need. Now you have to find them. You can break this activity into a couple of different areas:

- leveraging of your existing contacts
- research.

Leverage Your Existing Contacts. The best way for you to generate names of prospects is to talk to people you already know. Start with your existing customers. Your best referral is from one of your current customers who refers you to a prospect. (It's a lot better if your current customer actually knows someone there, and it's best if your customer contacts that person first. However, even a list of names is helpful.)

You are looking for the following:

- **Other customers like your current customer**—This assumes that you are asking for referrals from customers you define as "good." Many times, people leave one customer and go somewhere else in the same industry. Sometimes, they stay in contact with former coworkers. Follow the people you know when they leave.

- **Suppliers to your customer**—Depending on the kinds of business in your account portfolio, your customer's suppliers also may be prospects. A customer recommendation here is very powerful because the customer has some power over suppliers.

- **Your customer's customers**—Again, depending on your account portfolio, your customer's customers also may be good prospects.

- **Your customer's competitors**—In retail, this is a no-brainer. And it's true as well for every other type of sales situation. If your customer buys, the customer's competitors also buy . . . and some of your old customers may work there.

Make it your goal to have a conversation with your best contacts inside your best customers and ask them for referrals.

Another source of prospects is right inside your organization. Warehouse people, financial managers, service technicians, and other distribution salespeople may have suggestions and contacts for prospective customers. Ask around.

Other "people" sources include your vendors and noncompetitive salespeople. Sometimes your better vendors can make suggestions based on what they have seen in the industry. Also, make it a point to introduce yourself to other salespeople you meet when calling on customers. If they're not competitors but are calling on one of your best accounts, they also may be calling on other accounts to which you'd like to sell. Offer to swap lists with those sales reps and see if you can do some joint calls where you introduce each other to a few of the better prospects.

Research. Then, there's the research area. A good research starter list includes

- **industrial directories**—check local directories, not just the big ones.

- **the Internet**—type in a few keywords that describe what you're looking for, and see what comes up.

- **lead-generation people**—some Internet and software companies offer this service.

- **the telephone book**—yep, they're all in there.

- **chambers of commerce and other local business groups**—the local retail people tend to be there.

- **purchased lists**—trade publications, newspapers, and industry newsletters sometimes sell their lists of contacts.

- **smoke-stacking trips**—otherwise known as driving around and looking for stuff; this is not a prime sales time activity.

- **tradeshows**—don't focus only on the ones where you exhibit. Do your customers attend local tradeshows? Maybe you should, too. You may be able to generate a nice list of your customers' competitors. Maybe you could sell them something.

Here's an important piece of research: When you have identified some prospects, you need to do a little research specifically on them. Identify their potential because what you know of it will drive how much time you're willing to spend trying to get in the door. Do as much of this as you can before you visit or call them. You really need to establish some sort of rule of thumb for potential that you can get without a lot of effort. The easiest way to do this is to start with a current customer you know pretty well. You know what you sell that customer. What else do you know? How many employees does the customer have? How much square footage? What is the customer's annual sales total? Use the numbers you have to work back to some ratios. For example:

- Every 10 employees equals $20,000 of annual potential sales.

- The customer has $100 of annual potential sales for every 10 square feet of space the customer occupies.

- For every $1 million the customer sells, there is $10,000 of annual sales potential for me.

If you have a simple method for checking potential, you can save a lot of time. And remember that a lot of prospects won't answer the question, How much can you buy from me? They may answer it later, but you need to know *before* you spend a lot of time trying to crack the code.

Step 2: Identify/Qualify the Decision-Making Process

The second step in the sales process (and the second part of prospecting) is to identify/qualify the DMP. Previously, we talked about the two key questions:

1. Who is involved?
2. How does it work?

In this section, we're going to take a much deeper look at this part of the sales process—beginning with *why* identifying and qualifying people is important:

- **People = Opportunities.** If you review a list of people you know, you'll probably find that you know more people inside your best accounts. Looks like a chicken-and-egg scenario—do you know more people there because you do a lot of business, or do you do a lot of business because you know more people there? Research has shown that there is a correlation between the number of contacts you have and the number of opportunities on which you get to work. In a new account, you need at least one good contact to get the ball rolling. In an existing account, you may need to find some more people to sell that account a fuller range of products. One distributor did an annual analysis to calculate the average number of contacts for the top 20 accounts in each territory. The distributor then set an annual goal to increase the number of contacts in each account by 1. So, where the beginning number was 3 (60 contacts/20 accounts), the distribution salesperson's goal was to move that number to 4 over the course of the year. That meant identifying and calling on 20 new people inside the top 20 accounts. Not so shocking, sales tended to go up faster in the territories where the salespeople added the highest numbers of new contacts.

- **People = Checkability.** New concept, new word. *Checkability* means your ability to get information from more than one source. The customer's engineer you're working with says the project is going to be complete by January. The customer's salesperson you're also working with says that if it's not ready by December, the organization won't be able to roll it out at the tradeshow in February. How real are those claims? What kind of decisions would you make if you only talked to the engineer? You might decide that this opportunity is "real" and waste a lot of time. By also involving the customer's salesperson as a separate information source, you get a much better picture of reality, and you can make an informed decision on how much time to spend on this opportunity.

- **People = Protection.** How many people are defending your business when you're not there? Ideally, there is a minimum of three people at each of your accounts doing that. The reason: 99% of all salespeople (in this case, your potential competitors) give up when they have to work with three people to get a piece of business. How many people need to change their minds before you lose a piece of business?

Who Do You Want or Need to See?

Think about the products that you sell. Think about where you are effective selling them. Who are the people involved in the process? What are their job titles? Note that you might need to call on different people to sell different things. Here's a list of possibilities:

- architects
- buyers
- contractors
- counter salespeople in retail operations
- crew members/supervisors
- engineering staff/supervisors
- finance people/supervisors
- installers/supervisors
- logistics people/supervisors
- maintenance staff/supervisors
- marketing, sales, and customer service people/supervisors
- owners
- production staff/supervisors
- product managers
- procurement personnel/supervisors
- quality staff/managers

- safety staff/managers
- senior management
- store managers
- warehouse staff/supervisors.

Look at the list above (and maybe add a few other relevant job titles). How many of these people should you know at key accounts? How many of them do you know? Where are the gaps? A good assignment for you this year is to add names of new people on whom you're calling.

A handy tool to help drive your people-prospecting efforts is the contact matrix. Here is an example, with some strategic contact levels and sample departments filled in:

	Maintenance	Production	Purchasing
Management			
Supervisor			
Doer			

To create your own matrix for some organizations you're calling on, you might want to add another level of contacts (such as calling on managers in addition to the staff). Remember that the more people you call on, the more opportunities you're likely to find, and the more secure your business is within that customer.

At a *minimum,* you want to have one contact in three different parts of the organization—one at each strategic level. Here's an example of how such a matrix might look:

	Maintenance	Production	Purchasing
Management	B. Jones		
Supervisor		J. Smith	
Doer			P. Brown

A true distribution sales pro will begin by trying to fill in the entire matrix—and then will add other department columns—for the most important customers. This matrix helps you visualize where you're missing contact and where you're missing opportunities.

How Do You Get to Those People? Many salespeople take a one-size-fits-all approach to contacts. If the purchasing officer wants to see a line card, then maybe everyone wants to see a line card. If the lead on a plumbing crew wants to see a field demo, then maybe everyone wants to see how the product actually works. But, not so fast. . . .

Keep this in mind as you try to set up an appointment with someone new: Different people care about different things. And job roles tell us a lot about what might be useful to different people. Here are some examples:

- Owners and senior managers tend to be concerned about the profitability of the organization. When you attempt to talk with these people, show them that you have thought about ways to help them become more profitable. A brochure or line card is not as helpful here as a list of 10 projects you have worked on that have helped people improve the profitability of their operations.

- Plant management is more focused on issues such as throughput (moving it faster through the facility), changeover/downtime (times when the process is not working), quality (rework, scrap, and warranty costs), and occasionally inventory. (A side note about inventory: there are three types—raw, work in process, and finished.) When trying to get to these people, you need to show them how you have solved problems.

- Engineering has two parts—design engineering (which designs new products) and plant engineering (which helps the plant run better).

- Maintenance is concerned with reducing maintenance costs—although these are not always the best people to go to when reducing cost means getting rid of maintenance employees.

- Purchasing often is held accountable for purchase price variance (buying it cheaper than last time), stock outs (not having what's needed), and inventory (having too much of what's needed).

- Quality assurance is concerned primarily with rework, scrap, and warranty costs, although personnel in this department occasionally will get involved with process design.

- Safety specialists are concerned with health, safety, and environmental issues.

- Risk management departments are relatively new and tend to be focused on reducing the organization's exposure in a wide range of areas, including insurance.

- Finance people are concerned with money, but they also often drive cost-reduction efforts within an organization. If you have a great idea for taking power costs down by 20%, they may be the first people who need to hear it. (But they are the last people who need to see your line card.)

If you're selling to retail operations, you might be able to touch a lot of those issues—and the good news is that they might not have thought about them or made strategic connections. For example, store managers may not know they can sell more product by making their business safer.

There are other parts of many organizations, and a lot of organizations are very simple: there's an owner, and there are a few employees. In a case like that, you may think that getting to the owner is enough; but even there, get to know at least one of the employees so that person can support you as you try to convince the owner to do something differently. A lot of good ideas are never implemented because the owner relies on input from Sweet Old Bill, and you ignored him when you were in there.

Professional distribution salespeople not only know they need to get in front of the right people; they also learn the right things to talk about when they get there. The worst thing is finally to get an audience with the owner and then have nothing to say (nothing the owner cares about). Know your audience, and use concepts and language that are relevant to set and conduct appointments.

What Do You Need to Know about Them?

The final issue that you need to address is the actual qualification process. You go into a meeting with a new person under the assumption that the person is either the decision maker or an influencer. To verify that assumption, you need to use that first appointment to get as much clarity as you can on the following questions:

- How much potential exists at this customer?
- Does this customer pay the bills?
- Who is involved in the DMP?
- How does the process work?

Wouldn't it be nice if you could just ask those four questions and get honest answers? Yep, but it doesn't often happen that way, so you need some methods other than bluntness.

One way to address this is to ask the person you're meeting with some things about the company that you can't get through research. A really good question is, What are you trying to accomplish? The person's ability to answer this question not only tells you about what is really important to that person; it also gives you insight into this person's authority level. Having no idea what the goals of the organization are suggests the person may not be involved in the DMP. (Sometimes the owners don't have clear goals. This gives you a great opportunity to introduce some new concepts to them. And when they start thinking about new things, you have a better chance to convert them to your solution. Think about a retail example where the store owner has no idea how much revenue a good store gets from every square foot of display space.)

Another good question is, What is your fiscal year? For bigger organizations, this is important; for the small retail business, it might not matter. But if the organization is big enough to do a formal business plan and budget, you want to know what the time frame is, so you can be involved in helping the organization create the plan. (This puts you way over in TAC.) Again, if the person cannot answer this question, it's a clue to the person's sophistication or decision-making authority.

You also can ask how the person is measured. You're looking for metrics of some sort so you can begin to present your ideas in ways that make sense to the customer. For example, if you learn that the company is trying to reduce warranty costs by 10%, you probably would tie the product you want to sell to that goal. Again, if the person you're meeting with can't tell you the goals or metrics of the organization, you may be learning something about that person's role in buying your product. (This also may be a great opportunity for you to educate this person about some things you have learned through your experience in the industry.)

You also want to define the process the customer follows in deciding to use a new distributor or a new product. Remember the question you ask: How does that work? You're more likely to get a clear picture of the role your contact plays in purchasing if you get an answer to this question.

You also are interested in getting some sense of the organization's potential and financial strength. You would get the answer to the question of potential by asking about sales figures, number of employees, square footage, or some other thing that you have learned to tie into sales dollars. The financial-strength part is trickier. To get all the formalities out of the way so the first order will go through smoothly, one sales pro gives the customer a credit application on the first call. You may not be that bold, but you need to ask a few questions about the length of time the company has been in business (even if the Web site tells you) and how long the prospect has worked with its key customers and distributors. If your contact is unwilling to have this kind of discussion, the person may be expressing discomfort with the topic. And there might be a good reason.

A lot of change would not be a good sign: turning over a lot of distributors or customers might be a signal that things are not going well.

The Prospecting Process

By now you've figured out that there is a process for everything—and prospecting is no exception. The best prospecting calls are not "cold." A lot of people recommend cold calls, and there are times when you have to do them; but they're not as effective as "lukewarm" calls.

A lukewarm prospecting process looks like this:

- **Pick a market niche that you plan to go after.** Examples might be hospitals, hair stylists, or residential roofing contractors. Learn everything you can about those enterprises. Spend some time reading a few articles from their trade journals. What are

---

PUTTING IT ALL TOGETHER

A distributor sales pro who worked for a fastener distributor needed some new customers. She also needed to have some way to decide where she should spend her time. She started the process by reviewing her current best customers. She noted that most of her good customers were in the steel erection/fabrication area, had a minimum of 10 employees, and had been in business for at least 25 years.

Using these criteria, she quickly was able to put together a list of the best prospects. She ended up with a short list of 12 "good" prospects. Because of her focus, she was able to convert 5 of these into customers within 90 days, and another 2 came on board by the end of another 90 days. During that six-month period, her sales increased by 25%—with most of the growth coming from those new customers.

---

the hot topics in the industry? Learn a few of the buzzwords so you can talk their talk when you do get to meet them.

- **Create a clear value proposition.** Answer the question, Why should a hospital switch from the current distributor to me? Remember our previous discussion about not wanting to use phrases like "quality" or "service"? Get real. Answer the question like this: "A hospital should switch to this product because it will save them 10 minutes per patient in changing the bedclothes." A retail answer might go something like this: "By switching to our product, this customer can increase sales from $12 per square foot to $28 per square foot per week in the portion of the store allotted to sales of pet food."

- **Develop some references/proofs.** A reference can be either the name of someone a prospect can call or something said by a current customer that has been documented in written form. Here's an example: "After working with Mary at ABC Hospital, we were able to save 40 hours per week in changing patients' bedclothes. This meant that we could provide the same amount of patient care in a week with one less person." If you are making a statement about quality ("Our parts last longer"), you need to have some evidence that supports the statement.

- **Do some research on each organization.** Almost everyone has a Web page or a listing in some sort of directory. What do they say about themselves? Learn what you can before you ask for an appointment.

- **Decide which job titles you need to call on to present your value proposition.** Then get their names so you can ask for those people specifically, rather than asking for "the purchasing manager." That kind of uncertainty is a dead giveaway that you don't know what you're doing.

- **If possible, make a survey call first.** If you can visit them easily, do so. Don't try to sell them anything. Just look around and maybe ask a few questions. One sales pro introduces himself to the prospect and says that he wants to learn a little about the business; and if he can add value, he'll call back and ask for an appointment. Some customers really appreciate that approach. You need to find the name of at least one person who might be the "right" sales target.

- **Send something before you ask for an appointment.** Dig around and find the name of the suspected key decision maker(s). Send them a first-class mailing (literally first-class mail, not just really good looking)—maybe include your brochure or line card, maybe not. Introduce yourself and your company; highlight a few examples where you have helped similar businesses increase sales or profits or reduce costs; then give a time when you intend to call for an appointment. Finally, call exactly at that time and try to schedule a "real" appointment.

This method doesn't always work, but it works at a much higher percentage than a straight cold call. Remember, you have only one chance to make a good first impression. Make sure that you do everything you can to differentiate yourself, beginning with your first encounter with the customer.

Here's a seldom-used, but very effective, prospecting tip: talk to sales or customer service people first. One of the best ways to get into any organization is through the sales or customer service function. This is the unguarded gate of the castle. They can be valuable allies in helping you find the right people, and often they will tell you what's happening inside the company so that you go in with the right approach—from the beginning.

Earlier, you decided how much of your time needs to be spent on prospecting. Do a quick calendar review. As of right now, how many prospecting activities are on your calendar? To be effective, you always need to have some step 1 and step 2 activities on your calendar—with the right organizations.

Conclusion

Sales shares similarities with "manufacturing equipment." In production, you recognize that if you don't put something into the front of the machinery, there is no way that you can get anything out at the back end. In distributor sales, the back end of the machine is the order. The front end is the prospecting process. You need a continuous focus on identifying and qualifying new customers and identifying and qualifying additional decision makers. Failure to put your focus on those two things consistently will cause the machine to shut down.

FOLLOW-UP ASSIGNMENTS

1. Establish prospecting goals for the next 30 days. Answer these questions:
   - How many prospecting calls will you make?
   - How many new people will you find?
   - How much potential will you identify in that period of time?

2. Fill out a contact matrix (like the one in exhibit 5-4) for your top three customers. See what it tells you.

3. Call on your top three customers, and ask for referrals.

4. Do a minimum of one hour's research into the resources you have, and identify some new customers.

5. Construct a list of the existing customer organizations in which you intend to identify new people to give yourself a chance to sell them some different products.

6. Construct a list of the job titles for the new people you need to find.

7. Put together a list of the new prospects that you intend to call on within the next 30 days. Identify the job titles you need to call or visit.

8. Do a minimum of one hour of research on at least three of your target prospects *before* you make the first call. Write down what you learn. Do this research during non-sales prime time (Monday–Friday, before 7 a.m. or after 5 p.m., or on weekends).

Creating (and Finding) Opportunities

Before you begin, answer these questions:

1. How many sales calls within the last month had a stated goal of finding a new piece of business? And how many times was the customer aware of that goal, in advance of the call?

2. How many times were you successful? How many new pieces of business did you find? What was their value? How many of these pieces of business did the customer volunteer? How many of these did you create?

3. How many opportunities were for new rather than existing customers? How many of them were for focus products? How many met your "good order" definition?

4. How many opportunities have a defined + *something else*?

5. How many opportunities have a specific, scheduled next step?

6. How many opportunities are being evaluated currently by your customers? How many new opportunities moved into the qualification stage during the last month? How clear are you on what those customers are seeking?

7. Over the past 30 days, how many objections did you get? What were the objections?

A lot of sales pros think selling begins at the next two steps in the sales process—they find a piece of business and then do what they think is necessary to get a chance to quote it. Most of the heavy lifting in distributor sales occurs here—but if you have not done the first two steps correctly, you're probably wasting time identifying opportunities and working in the customer's qualification process.

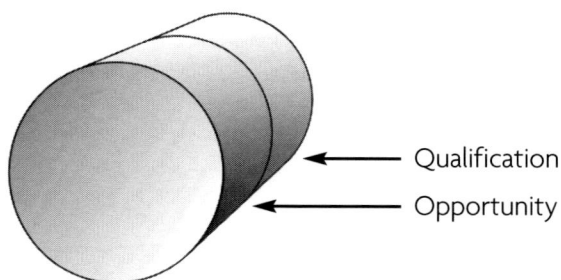

Qualification

Opportunity

Step 3: Identify/Qualify the Opportunity

Selling is tough, but some things are very simple: To get an order, you first have to find an opportunity. Without having a piece of business to work on, you have nothing. A lot of salespeople are guilty of being too customer-centric. They focus on the relationship with the customer, hoping that a good relationship will produce opportunities. Top-level pros care about the relationship because it's the incubator; but every time they speak with a customer, they're looking for a piece of business that they have a chance to book.

Two very obvious things need to be restated here:

- You can't get an opportunity if you're not dealing with a qualified customer.

- You can't get an order if you're not dealing with the decision maker(s).

So, to be effective, you have to have finished steps 1 and 2 of the process before you move into step 3.

Definition of a Real Opportunity (Again)

You have heard it often enough to be able to say it in your sleep: Real sales opportunity = Product/service you are selling + Something else.

Let's look at a practical application of this basic sales equation. You work for a bearing distributor, and you uncover an opportunity to quote a bearing that you stock. The customer always has bought this bearing from your competitor. You were lucky enough to call on a day when the purchasing agent had a requisition on the desk and needed a quote. The customer asked if you had the item in stock and what it costs. You told the customer you had it, and you gave a price. Now you're waiting by the phone hoping for a call and a purchase order. Hear any crickets?

Many distribution salespeople think the equation in that example looks like this:

Real sales opportunity = Bearing + Lower cost.

But, in reality, if you quoted a low number, the purchasing agent will take your number to the original distributor and use it as a club to beat down that distributor's price. That's what happens a lot of the time.

Some circumstances might have changed that likely sequence:

- Competitor didn't have it in stock; *your solution:* Bearing + In stock.

- Competitor didn't offer an extended warranty; *your solution:* Bearing + Extended warranty.

- Customer wanted to lower power costs and was willing to consider a different bearing; *your solution:* Bearing + Lower power costs.

In each of those circumstances, you can see that the equation was proved out. You need to find something to add to the product or service that you are selling if you are trying to take the sale away from the competition. As you look for opportunities, keep that simple rule in the back of your mind. When you find an opportunity, ask yourself this question: What is the + *something else*? If you're unsure of the answer, take time to figure it out (or at least acknowledge that this may not be a real opportunity for you).

Find Opportunities or Create Them

Opportunities come in two flavors: those you find and those you create. Order takers count on *finding* pieces of business. Distribution sales pros are happy to find them, too, but they're more interested in *creating* them. The good news from the sales front is that the more effective you are in creating opportunities, the more opportunities you tend to find, as well.

There is a sales hierarchy for opportunities. The higher you go, the more time will be spent working on the opportunity; but on the flipside, you add more value, and two things become more likely—booking the order and doing so at a decent margin.

Level 1. This is the lowest level of the hierarchy. The customer has purchased a product/service from you previously and calls again to ask for pricing and availability. Customers who do this are the ones we like best. You're very likely to get the order. If a competitor is aware of the opportunity, however, that salesperson may be used against you, and your margins may tend to erode over time.

Here's an example: You have been selling your customer beauty supplies. The customer, needing more of a product, calls and asks you about pricing and availability. You confirm the product is in stock and that the price paid the last time is still good. There's no need to create a + *something else* here because you're the incumbent and likely to get the order. Looks a lot like order taking.

Level 2. The customer previously has purchased a product or service from your competitor, but is unhappy with that distributor or the distributor's salesperson. Either you call the customer or the customer calls you because the customer is interested in doing something differently. This is really nice because you have a good chance to get the order and take it away from the competitor. You may have to be aggressive in your pricing, but you can handle it.

Here's an example: The last three times that the customer ordered pipe from your competitor, the pipe showed up either late or with pieces missing. The purchasing agent wants to buy from someone else—at the very least to wake up the current distributor—and would consider switching all of the business to you if you perform and the previous distributor continues to fail. The + *something else* here would be your ability to sell the pipe + *on time and complete.* Transactions at this level look like sales, but because the customers do all the heavy lifting, they still get chalked up in the order-taking column.

Level 3. A customer previously has purchased a needed product or service from your competitor. The buyer knows that there's a problem but won't tell you about it because of some loyalty to the current distributor. Getting these kinds of orders is both challenging and fun. You have to make two sales here. Before you book the order, your first sale is getting the prospect to acknowledge the gap between what's needed and what's being delivered, without making the customer feel angry or stupid. You can get this order, and you might not have to be the cheapest.

Here's an example of level 3: A prospect has been buying valves from your competitor, and there have been some quality issues that have required a lot of unpaid warranty work for their clients. Through careful questioning, you discover the recent high levels of unpaid repair; and the customer decides to buy the next set of valves from you in an effort to reduce that cost. The + *something else* here would be your ability to sell the valves + *less unpaid warranty work.* This is the first level at which you definitely can declare yourself a salesperson. This is not order taking because the customer was not aware of the significance of the warranty costs until you pointed them out.

Level 4. A customer needs a product, but doesn't know it. The buyer is used to a certain quality or service level—provided by a competing distributor from whom the customer always gets the product—and isn't aware that real alternatives are available. You go in, help the buyer uncover a problem, document the value of solving the problem, and begin getting orders.

Here's a level 4 example: The customer is buying motors from your competitor at a price lower than you can sell them. You know that the only way your competitor can offer that price is by selling the motors in larger quantities than the customer really needs. You meet with the purchasing agent and share information on the amount of inventory carried by an "average" customer. As a result, the purchaser determines that the current inventory is $20,000 greater than it should be. You show the decision maker how paying a little more for your motors, but holding fewer of them on the shelf, will help reduce inventory costs by about $15,000 over the next six months—and improve cash flow. The customer not only orders motors from you, but also invites you to look at other areas where inventory may be reduced. The + *something else* here is your ability to sell the motors + *$15,000 less inventory over six months.* When you book this order, you have reached the pinnacle of professional selling.

See how this level 4 selling also ties in with the earlier discussions of total acquisition cost versus per unit cost? In the example, your PUC was higher than the competitor's—but the TAC savings were fairly dramatic. By redefining the customer's problem from "I need to buy cheaper motors" to "I need to carry less inventory," you give yourself a chance to win big because you're involved at the trigger point where the opportunity is created. In fact, *you* create it. At each of the other three levels, the customer drives most of the action, and your involvement occurs later in the process where the ability-to-influence line is below the price/availability line.

Finally, let's look at a retail example. The customer is a store owner who is buying some of the products sold in the store from your competitor. The customer currently is getting about five inventory turns per year. In this case, the store stocks $20,000 worth of products and gets $100,000 of sales per year. You know that the industry average is seven turns per year. The store should be getting $140,000 worth of sales for its $20,000 stocking level. You show the owner how to rearrange in-store displays (using your products this time). The owner agrees to try your ideas and buys from you. The store's sales improve, and you get orders for more and more items because you not only sell products, but also show the owner how to merchandise those items. Your + *something else* is products + *merchandising consulting.*

The opportunities that you find are influenced by two things:

1. **Who you talk with**—As you try to find opportunities, don't forget the importance of talking with the right people. To clarify, different people control different opportunities in different organizations. In the last chapter, you saw how different job titles had different interests. When you're looking for opportunities, you have to match up the proposed solutions that you're trying to sell with the people who might care. Examples of this would be presenting power-saving options to either plant engineering or plant management rather than to the maintenance department. Your solution for reducing inventory might be presented

more effectively to someone in finance or materials management than to someone in the plant because plant personnel believe inventory allows them to run less efficiently. In a retail venue, presenting a higher number of turns per square foot of space to the owner or product manager would be more effective than presenting it to the purchasing department.

2. **What you talk about**—We've been talking about this for a while now—and you can see the value. Without belaboring the point (too much), if you want to have discussions about reducing the customer's TAC, you should not call on purchasing and ask for an opportunity to quote to show how low your prices are. And when you're calling on the maintenance manager, it might be better to show how your product can be used by less-trained people than to talk about how your product will eliminate three maintenance positions.

Look at the calls you have scheduled. On whom are you calling? Are all of your calls on engineering or purchasing departments? Should you be calling on different people to sell different products? What are the topics you're covering? Are you making pretty much the same presentation every place you go—or are you talking about the right things with the right people?

The Seven Diagnostic Questions

Remembering our road analogy from chapter 4, you know the importance of getting "yes" or "no" answers to almost every question you ask so that you can determine whether to spend more time on a given customer, person, or piece of business. This really is important when you find a piece of business you want to pursue.

You're not trying only to find something that you're interested in, but also trying to find out how important it is to the customer. (If you did your job well in step 2 of the sales process, you spent some time talking with customers about their goals and metrics. You should have a pretty good idea of these, but you need a way to verify what you think you know.) You can use a questioning process to verify that an opportunity is real. You don't need to do this on recurring pieces of business that you get from your existing customers; but if you're trying to sell something to someone who never has bought it before—or to a prospect who never has bought anything from you—you need to go through the questions presented here and see what they tell you.

Question 1: What Is the Application? This is the most basic sales question of all. You need to know how the product or service will be used. This will help you ensure you are proposing what the buyer really needs versus what the buyer might ask for. (Remember that customers tend to ask only for what they currently use. Sometimes they don't ask for the right thing.) If the customer is unwilling or unable to tell you how the product or service will be used, it's a red flag. You might not be dealing with the decision maker, or the opportunity might not be real for you.

Question 2: Is This Expense Already Budgeted or Approved? The answer to this question could be good news or bad news. If the answer is "yes," you can assume that the buyer has money. But considering that the buyer got a number approved without talking to you, it's possible that a decision to use a competitor already has been made. A "no" answer might be good because it could indicate that you're getting a chance to help define what the buyer needs. On the other hand, it might mean that there is a budgetary process going on where no real opportunity exists—at least for now. In the worst case, the customer is either unwilling or unable to answer the question. You know what that means.

Question 3: How Many Do You Need? This question is not always applicable but when it is, it tells you a lot. A good answer is an exact number: We need a case. You might want to follow up with a "why?" question, but at least the need seems to be defined. When the answer is a range, watch out: "1, 5, 50, or 100" is another red flag for you. It could mean this call is an unfunded fishing expedition. The wider the spread on quantity, the less real the opportunity tends to be. Again, the decision maker knows how much is needed; other people don't.

Question 4: Who Is the Competition, and Is It the Incumbent? You ask this question to ensure that you know against what you're being compared. Are we talking apples and apples or apples and pomegranates? You also need to know if the competition is the current distributor. If so, that salesperson has the inside track unless there have been a lot of mistakes or problems. The worst answer to this question? You guessed it—either "I don't know" or "You don't need to know." Either one of those casts doubt on the authority of the person, the reality of the opportunity, or both.

Question 5: What Is Your Target Price Range? Don't get the target price range question confused with this question: What is the competitive bid? Here you're asking for a range of acceptable pricing. You need to check that range with your understanding of the application to make sure that the comparisons are real. Many distribution salespeople are afraid to ask this question. Be more afraid if you don't. You are trying to discern if the customer wants to have enough dialogue with you to give you a reasonable chance to get the order. If the buyer doesn't trust you enough to give you a price range, will there be enough trust to give you the order? Again, if there is an unwillingness to share this information, the prospect is telling you a lot about your chances of winning the order.

Question 6: When Do You Need It? Some opportunities that look real become very unreal when you learn the time frame. The answer that you're looking for, however, is a definite date. When people plan to buy something, they know when they want to buy it. If they can't give you a time frame, they're telling you a few things that you want to pick up on: you're not dealing with the decision maker(s), or the opportunity is not (yet) real.

Question 7: Why Would You Consider Using a Different Distributor? This is a powerful question because it gets to the heart of the matter. You're *not* asking, Where do I need to be to get the business? Instead, you're trying to get insight into the customer's decision-making process. The most common answer today is, "A cheaper price." Generally, however, that's not the only factor. If the person you're speaking with can't answer the question, be prepared to help answer it or forget about getting the business (if you're not the incumbent).

• • •

Those questions are powerful mainly because they may open the door to a real discussion with the customer. You're not only gathering answers—although the answers are critically important; you also are checking the validity of the potential piece of business. If a person you're questioning generally is unwilling or unable to answer the questions, your chances of booking an order there are slim to none. For that reason, it's important that you not fill in the blanks and assume you know any of the answers. You are looking for the interaction. Some research indicates that your likelihood of booking an order increases with each answer that you get. In how many of the opportunities you're working on right now are you unsure of many or most of the answers to those questions?

Define the Next Step

The most powerful (and simplest) way to check on the reality of an opportunity is to try to schedule a next step on every piece of business that you find. As an example, let's say you've just discovered that a customer needs some floorcovering and wants to look at samples. You show some samples and then ask, "When can I call you to see which samples you like best?" The customer can move the answer in a lot of directions, but the one you want to hear sounds like "Tomorrow afternoon at 3" or "I'll be here at 10 a.m. on Tuesday." Any vague answer ("In a few days," "Next week, sometime," or the worst, "I'll call you if I'm interested") should alert you that you have a problem. We'll talk more about this concept when we discuss sales calls.

Step 4: Identify/Qualify the Customer's Qualification Process

When you've identified (or created) an opportunity, the need for proactivity changes. Until this part of the process, the customer or prospect may be fairly passive. The only things the buyer has had to do so far is give you an opportunity to call or meet and maybe answer a few questions.

When a piece of business is defined, the customer has to do something. (This explains why a lot of people don't like to see salespeople—sales reps actually make them work.)

When a customer agrees to consider buying something from you, that person has to go through some sort of process to answer this question: Do I believe that the solution offered by [*your name*] at [*your company's name*] meets my needs?

The process may be quick, or it may be long and involve many people. As a distribution salesperson, you need to know as much about this process as you can *before* you get into it. One label that can be applied to this step of the sales process is the "Black Hole of Selling." In physics, a black hole is part of the universe so dense that not even light can escape from it. Many opportunities disappear into the black hole of qualification and never come out again.

The Three Things the Customer Qualifies

When you read the customer's qualifier question ("Do I believe that the solution offered by [*your name*] at [*your company's name*] meets my needs?"), you see that the customer qualifies three things: product/service, company, and salesperson.

Product/Service. This is the factor we deal with most easily. We know that people like to get samples and evaluate them. They also need to see demonstrations of how things work. There are times when the customer must see technical specifications and test results. The aspects of this factor are tangible, and we know that we're providing them. What makes product and service even easier to deal with is that we often learn exactly what's being sought by the questions the customer asks: Does this meet x standard? How long will it work before it needs to be replaced or lubricated?

There may be some very formal processes here, such as getting your product on the print or drawing or on a formal bill of materials. And you may need to get your company on an approved vendor list. Other times, the process may be informal—"Let's show this to Fred in maintenance. If he likes it, we'll buy it."

When someone is evaluating your product or service, there are a couple of questions that you need to ask:

- What are you currently using? *(apples to apples, again)*

- What results are you currently getting? *(to make sure your product can do the job)*

- What kind of improvement are you looking for? *(to be certain you can help them)*

- What kind of evaluation are you going to do? *(to learn their process)*

- When will the evaluation be complete? *(a reality check—the shorter the time frame, the greater the prospect's interest in working with you).*

As always, you're looking to drive some sort of dialogue with the customer. If someone is willing to take the time to answer the questions you ask, that person is probably at least considering your solution. If not, you have a problem.

Company. The customer's second evaluation involves your employer. The buyer may love the product and at least tolerate you, but if that person lacks confidence in the organization you're working for, you won't get the order. Find out what the purchasing agent needs to know about your company. Some things are simple—credit and freight policies. Some things are more complex—quality standards and financial health. Perhaps approved vendor lists or facility audits are involved. In other circumstances, it may be as simple as giving the buyer the names of some of your other customers.

To be effective, you need to remember that buyers do care about the company they're dealing with, and they may want to know more than your brochure or Web site tells them. It would be good to ask, What do you need to know about your potential distributors? and let them tell you. (Over time, if prospects give you similar answers, begin assembling your own informal sheet of frequently asked questions and provide some of what you think they need to know as part of your sales presentations.

Salesperson. Yes, it really is all about you. At some point, the customer asks the question, Do I want to buy from this person? In the old days, the assumption was that salespeople had to be likable to win orders. Hence, the stereotypical salesperson who is a jolly joke teller wearing a plaid sports jacket. At some level, there is truth in that—but likability is less important today than it was in earlier times. Customers want salespeople who add value. Do you make your buyers' jobs easier? Are you helping them earn a bonus? Keep that job? Get promoted?

You want to demonstrate that you're valuable because the feeling will rub off on both the products/services you sell and the company for which you work. Surveys of customers have ranked items such as problem-solving and follow-up skills as having greater importance than product knowledge or integrity. Those findings tell you something about how you should present yourself. Think about the statement you make when you are 15 minutes late for an appointment. The customer thinks the distribution salesperson is unreliable, so the product and the company may be unreliable as well.

Unfortunately, this also is the hardest kind of evaluation to get your arms around. Very few companies actually provide grades to sales reps. You need to work on creating a "brand" for you. What can customers count on when dealing with you? Does it add value? Does it differentiate you from all the other distribution salespeople who call on them?

Objections You Encounter

An offshoot of the qualification process is the objection. An objection normally occurs when there is a gap between what the customer expects and what the customer perceives you are offering. An example could involve delivery. Your truck delivers to the customer's area every Wednesday. The competitor has daily deliveries. An objection here could take a lot of different forms:

- "You guys aren't close enough to service our account."
- "We need deliveries within one day."
- "We'd have to carry a lot of inventory to buy from you guys."

Objections also occur for other reasons. The most common is the customer's desire to tell you "no" before spending any more time on the opportunity. A secondary reason is that the customer is setting you up for a price negotiation later.

The good news is that an objection often is a sign of customer interest. Someone who takes the time to show you the gap is offering you a chance to close that gap and make a sale. Don't fear objections; welcome them. Best case, you overcome the objection and book the order. Worst case, you quickly learn that you have no hope of booking the order, and move on to another opportunity that is more real for you.

Over the course of your career, you'll hear lots of different objections:

- credit terms (credit policies too tough)
- delivery (delivery times/accuracy)
- environmental (now more than ever)
- inventory (not enough)
- packaging (not delivered in ways that can be used easily)
- product breadth (not enough variety)
- product depth (not enough options on certain products)
- quality (doesn't work as well as competitor's product)
- safety (product might injure people)
- service (no local service)
- technical support (no local support)
- warranty (not enough coverage).

For each of those objections, you need to know

- how your product/service/organization really stacks up against the competition

- what evidence you have to counter the objection

- how that evidence should be presented.

The worst thing a salesperson can do when encountering an objection is to appear surprised and have no answer. If you haven't done so already, make up a list of frequent objections, and put together your responses. There probably are only a handful of objections that you get, so be prepared to deal with them.

The good news about these kinds of objections is that, in most case, they indicate some level of interest on the part of the customer. Objections give you an opportunity to prove them wrong—and to get the order.

The Dreaded Price Objection. As you read the list above, you were wondering, Where the heck is price on that list? It's the one I get all the time.

The price objection deserves its own special discussion because it's normally a different kind of objection. Without a doubt, this is the most common objection a salesperson will hear over the course of a career. This is true for the following reasons:

- **It's easiest to give.** When a potential buyer tells you your price is too high, it's difficult sometimes to challenge the point without calling the customer a liar—that's what you're doing if you ask to see the competitor's quote or the last invoice.

- **It's hardest to disprove.** Even if a buyer can't prove the objection is valid, it's tough for you to *disprove* what you're told.

People who don't have the authority to say "yes" can tell you "no" easily. Remember that lots of people out there have the authority to buy what they bought last time from the distributor they bought from last time, but not the authority to switch distributors. Rather than tell you this, they'll often just tell you that your price is too high.

People who don't really have a need may raise this objection. When you have failed to give them a reason to buy from you, or if they don't have a need right now, the easiest answer they can give you is that your price is too high.

If people want you to give them a low price so they can beat up their existing distributors, they'll tell you your price is too high. They're hoping you'll come back with a lower number they can use in negotiations with their current suppliers.

And, in some cases, the objection is true. Sometimes the price you quote is higher than what the buyer currently is paying. If you haven't defined the + *something else* that adds value to your product, your price truly will be too high.

What to Do about Price Objections. The best way to deal with a price objection is to avoid getting one. Easily said, but not so easily done. Here's what you can do:

- **Get involved earlier.** If you remember the previous discussions on value versus price, you recall that the earlier you get involved in an opportunity, the less likely you are to face a price objection. If you're always running into valid price objections, you might be talking to the wrong people about the wrong things. As an example, if you call on purchasing and tell the buyer the company should buy from you because you can offer deals, you're begging to be hit over the head with a big club. By always talking to purchasing people, you're focusing your sales presentation on price.

- **Don't lead with price.** Don't be suckered into giving out price information before you fully have defined what the customer needs. Too often, you talk about a product, and the customer asks, "How much is it?" You always have the option to say that you can't give a price—just yet—because you don't know exactly what's needed, or how much of it is needed, or when it's needed. The alternative is to give a very wide price range that includes both your cheapest product and your most expensive one, and then explain the value of some of the products you're selling.

When you receive a price objection, you still have options, but they're limited:

- Make a conditional concession.
- Try to redefine the need.
- Give up.

Before you decide which of those options to use, go over this quick mental checklist:

- Do I have a qualified customer? Is this an organization with which I'll continue to deal?

- Am I sure that I'm dealing with the decision maker?

- Do I have a real opportunity at this business?

- Am I qualified—or is this part of the qualification effort?

Your response to the price objection should be based on the answers to those questions. If you're dealing with a good customer or prospect—and you know that you're talking with the decision maker(s) and you have a real chance of booking the order—you handle the situation differently than you would if the answer to any of the above questions were "no."

PUTTING IT ALL TOGETHER

Dealing with the Price Objection. A salesperson who worked for a power transmission distribution company had an opportunity to quote on 20 small-horsepower motors. The salesperson did not do any work with this company, although there had been numerous calls on the company over the years. The salesperson was told that the company "burned up" about 20 motors every year in its production process, so it was looking for better pricing than it was getting from the current supplier. The company had decided to bid out the opportunity. The salesperson surmised that it would be necessary to bid the motors at about a 10% gross margin just to be considered, and it was likely that this price would be given to the incumbent distributor and that supplier probably would match it.

The salesperson correctly understood that the only way to win was to change the problem from "buying cheaper motors" to "buying motors that did not burn out." In a meeting with the production manager, the sales pro showed that the company had been using the wrong motor for the task. During the discussion, the salesperson explained how the price of the motor was the smallest cost to the organization and how the cost of downtime associated with motor failure was the real cost issue. Working with the production manager, the salesperson proposed replacing the current motors with motors better suited to the work and then further promised to replace, at no charge, any motors that burned out during the year.

The end result was that the salesperson got an order for more expensive motors—without having to bid. The production manager wanted to eliminate downtime, not buy cheaper motors. Because of the work the sales rep did on this opportunity, the salesperson's business went from zero dollars to more than $100,000 during the year.

So, back to your options for countering the price objection:

- **Make a conditional concession.** Never just drop the price. Doing so not only establishes a bad precedent, but also casts doubt on your integrity: If you could have quoted this at $6.50, why did you start at $9? If you make a price concession, add some condition: "At $6.50, you have to take two cartons" or "At $6.50, we have to charge you for freight." If you counter in this way, you are sending the message that lower price gets the buyer less value. You also are showing that you have integrity in the process.

- **Try to redefine the need.** Remember that when the customer has defined what is needed, your ability to succeed has been reduced dramatically. Distribution sales pros try to redefine the need: "Do you need pipe, or do you need a shrink-wrapped bundle of pre-cut pipe to show up exactly the day your crew hits the site?" If you truly understand what the customer is trying to accomplish (and you truly believe that your product is the customer's best choice), then make an effort to redefine the need as the product + *something else.* This will give you the opportunity to reposition your product and move toward a discussion of TAC rather than simply PUC.

- **Give up.** Sometimes your best option is to give up. If you have determined that there is no real opportunity, you simply stop. This doesn't mean that you are rude or behave badly or that you slam the door on the way out; it simply means you state that your price is your price for this opportunity. Sometimes the customer ultimately will reward you with an order because the goal was to see what could be squeezed out of you before giving you the order.

When it comes to any objection—especially price—it's really important to remember that you should get them before you formally have quoted (as part of the qualification process). Note that we're still talking about step 4 in the sales process. You have not given a quote or a proposal yet. This is where you want to get your objections—not after you have quoted.

Conclusion

These two steps of the sales process are where you need to do your best work. Although, it doesn't "feel" like it, most sales are lost in these two steps. To have a "real" quote and then to have a chance to close a piece of business, you need to have opportunities that have been qualified by the customer. Take the time required here to get more out of your sales efforts.

FOLLOW-UP ASSIGNMENTS

1. Set goals for what you intend to accomplish in the following areas during the next 30 days:
   - appointments to create new opportunities
   - total value of new opportunities defined
   - at target accounts (existing and new customers)
   - for focus products.

2. Review your goals versus your results on a weekly basis. Define how well or how poorly you're meeting your goals.

3. Estimate how many new products/services you'll move into the qualification stage this month.

4. Put together a response to the top three objections that you have heard during the last month.

Quotes, Proposals, and Closing Sales

Before you begin, answer these questions:

1. How much of your opportunity pipeline will move into step 5 (quotes and proposals) over the next 30 days?
2. How many of the opportunities will be for target accounts? For focus products?
3. For how many of your opportunities should you provide simple quotes? For how many should you prepare full-blown proposals?
4. How many of the quotes and proposals should be present - ed in person?
5. How many scheduled closing calls do you have during the next 30 days? How much value do those calls represent? What is your close ratio? How many of those opportunities do you expect to book during the next 30 days?
6. How many of your open quotes are for opportunities at target accounts? For focus products?
7. How many meet your "good order" definition?

The final two steps in the distributor sales process involve quotes and closing. If you've done the first four steps correctly, this is a great place to be.

Step 5: Present Quotes and Proposals

The fifth step in the distribution sales process involves quotes and pro-posals. This is the first part of the sales process that feels "concrete" to both the salesperson and the customer. For that reason, many people on

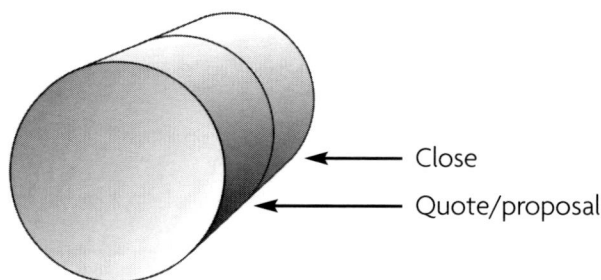

Close
Quote/proposal

both sides of the equation are in a big hurry to get here. Distribution salespeople want to get here because they think they're nearer to a sale, and customers want to get here to get it over with. But the true distribution sales pro only wants to get to this point of the sale if everything has been done correctly

Premature quoting is one of the biggest problems faced by all salespeople—but it's a real disaster for rookies. The problem with getting quotes out is that you have the illusion of doing something. There is no question that you have to do some kind of "quote" to get a sale, but the fallacy is that all of the quotes are valid.

As a salesperson, when you calculate your close ratio (Total $ quoted ÷ Total $ sold), you come up with a number. Here's an example: $1 million quoted ÷ $500,000 closed = 50% close ratio. You look at that number and say, I'm closing 50% of my quotes. You also "know" that you're losing a lot of quotes because the "price is too high"—an objection that relieves you of any feeling of responsibility because it's the company's fault, right?

The problem is that you never had a chance on a large number of the quotes you put out there because they were not real. You already have gotten a big dose of understanding reality, and you need to open up again because another big dose is coming. You lost a lot of your quotes for these reasons:

- The customer wasn't qualified. The buyer didn't have any money to spend on the product/service that you were offering, but wasn't likely to tell you that; it just happens. (*step 1 failure*)

- The person or people you were working with didn't have the authority to buy from you. Weird, but they never told you. *(step 2 failure)*

- The opportunity never existed for you. The customer was always going to buy from your competitor, or maybe had no money in the budget and was looking for budgetary numbers. *(step 3 failure)*

- Your product/service never made it out of the black hole of selling. Maybe it failed to meet the customer's needs, or maybe the customer just never got around to doing the kind of evaluation needed before buying from you. Either way, you had no chance. *(step 4 failure)*

Even worse news is that not all of the quotes you issue are real, so you may have a step 5 failure, too. (More on this later.)

The problem with selling is that in all of these cases—and many more—the sale appears to go forward. You continue to work as if you have a shot. The customer knows you don't, but never really comes out and says it because the quoting process is almost always valuable to the customer. At the very least, that person gets a confirmation that the price from the current distributor is around the market price. The customer also may get information needed to put together a budget. At the top end of the scale, the customer gets a club with which to bash the current distributors until they lower their prices to the ridiculous low-ball figure you offered in frustration over never being able to get an order from this customer.

As a distribution sales pro, you must guard against being in a big hurry to get to this part of the process. You want to get here as quickly as you can, but you don't want to get here unprepared. It does no good to reach the fire in two minutes only to discover you don't have a fire truck. That kind of speed is relatively worthless, right?

The distribution sales process is a series of sequential steps that must be done in order, every time. Do it the right way, and you may end up with a few less quotes—and a few more sales. More money for less effort—what a concept.

The Purpose of a Quote

In the introduction to the sales process, you learned that the purpose of a quote is to help the customer answer the following question: What are the distributors really offering?

In some cases, all of the information the customer needs to make an informed purchasing decision can be presented verbally—possibly over the phone. As an example, you have sold some wire to a customer over the last year. The customer needs more wire and calls you. The customer asks if you have the wire in stock and if the pricing is the same. You answer the questions, and the customer gives you a purchase order. This is the simplest case, but notice that the customer has to do it. If you have set the customer up with some sort of pricing matrix available over the Internet where the customer can check your stock and calculate the price, the salesperson has no part in the sale.

As you move into more complex sales or try to sell something new—either trying to sell an item to a new prospect or a new product to an existing customer—the quoting process becomes more complicated because the customer doesn't really know what you're offering. The buyer almost always needs to have your offer in writing. The written offer protects the buyer and documents the purchase decision within the buyer's organization.

You probably also want to provide the information in writing so there is no confusion later about the price you offered, the delivery date, or other issues that seem to come up even when it's in writing.

Depending on the complexity of the opportunity and the relationship that you have with the customer, the quote might include the following factors:

- product/service (description)
- quantity
- delivery
- terms
- warranty
- always the *force majeure* clause to cover you in case of freak typhoons.

Those are the elements of a quote. The customer needs to know what you and your organization are offering; and you tell the customer what you're offering, either informally (verbal) or more formally (written). If you give a quote, the customer should have all the information needed to make an informed buying decision.

The Five Bs of Quotes

When you think about quotes, you probably think that they are one of two types: *budget* and *buy.* In fact, there are five different types of quoting situations that you probably will run across in the course of a year. You need to recognize the type of situation you're in because the amount of time and effort you put into a quote should be connected with the type of quote that the situation requires.

Buy. The best kind of quote is a *quote for buy.* To qualify, you would have to know that the first four steps of the sales process have been completed successfully:

- You know that the customer is qualified.
- You know that you're dealing with the decision maker(s).
- You know that you have a real opportunity.
- You know that your product/service, your company, and you have been qualified by the customer.

The kicker is that the purchase time frame must be within the customer's current budget year. If all of those elements are present, you have a quote for buy.

Budget. The next best kind of quote is a *quote for budget.* To qualify, again, you would have to know that the first four steps of the sales process have been completed. The difference is that the purchase time frame is the customer's next budget year. Knowing the customer's fiscal year and planning cycle lets you distinguish between quoting something that the customer needs right now and something that the customer needs next year.

There is another kicker here. In step 3, the second of the seven diagnostic questions is, Is this expense already budgeted or approved? Because the answer to the question is "no" for the current time period, a quote for budget is really in step 3, not step 5. There is a very real possibility on a budgetary quote that you will have to go back and revisit steps 3 and 4, and you may end up requoting the opportunity before you get (or don't get) the order. Remember that a lot of budgeted items are not approved, so a budgetary quote can't be real until the approval is in place.

Bid-for-Bid. The third type of quote is a *bid-for-bid quote.* If you're dealing with contractors, this is a regular part of your day. They're bidding jobs and asking you for quotes. The most important thing for you to know here is whether you get the order if the contractor gets the job, or whether you're competing with other distributors for the order.

To qualify, you need to have completed the first four steps of the sales process. If the customer isn't sure that your product will work in the application the customer is bidding on, the product can't be purchased from you even if the customer gets the order.

Again, a bid-for-bid is really not a step 5 quote. Because the customer doesn't have a need unless an order is received, you don't have a real opportunity yet. You may end up requalifying and/or requoting, based on what happens with the customer, even if your buyer gets the order. This kind of quote is also in step 3.

Ballpark. The fourth kind of quote is a *ballpark quote.* The customer has some interest in working with you and is asking for pricing to see if you're in the ballpark. This kind of quote can occur anywhere in the sales process from step 1 to step 4, but real ballpark quotes occur predominantly in either step 2 or step 4. A step 2 ballpark quote occurs when no real opportunity is present, but the customer at least is considering working with another distributor. A step 4 ballpark quote really is part of the qualification process where the customer is checking your pricing as part of the decision-making process.

In either case, you'll be asked to requote. If it's a step 2 ballpark quote, you'll have to go back to step 3 and define an opportunity and then go through some sort of qualification process before you get to a step 5 quote.

Blow-off. The fifth (and worst) kind of quote is the *blow-off quote,* which can occur in many different circumstances. The customer may be checking a competitor's pricing or simply giving you a piece of business to quote to make you go away (happy). A blow-off quote is not anywhere in the sales process, and it's simply a waste of time for the distribution salesperson.

• • •

When you recognize what kind of quote you're dealing with, you need to make a conscious decision about how to deal with it. You might respond the same way to a ballpark quote or a budgetary quote as you would to a quote for buy if this is a key prospect. The only difference is that you know you're using the quote merely to open a dialogue with the customer, not to make a sale. In a blow-off situation, you may issue a quote, but you won't put the same time or effort into it—and you probably won't low-ball the price.

There are no easy ways to know how real the quoting opportunities are. Your goal is to get the information you need so that you can assess each opportunity. If the customer asks for a quote, have you done enough to distinguish between an actual "now" opportunity and a simple waste of your time?

Quotes versus Proposals

You may have noticed that the word that I use to describe the work of this step is *quote.* There is another word that describes a slightly different process: *proposal.* These words are not used interchangeably, although they both may occur in the fifth step of the sales process, because they're different tools to be used in different situations.

The simple process described above pertains to a quote. No matter how many pages it takes to translate it into legalese, a quote is simply a confirming document. You confirm a set of mutual obligations with the customer. That is, you will provide certain things if the customer takes the things at the price you offer. You use a quote when all the customer needs is confirmation of a few basic facts.

A proposal, however, is a selling document. Like a quote, it seeks to answer the customer's question, What is the distributor really offering? But it also tries to convince the customer that your proposed solution is the right one. A proposal looks different from a quote because it contains much more information. It probably will have more pages than a quote and may include photos, drawings, charts, and tables.

A typical proposal format might include the following elements:

- **An introduction describing the customer's problem/opportunity**—You might present a scenario that begins, "ABC Company, a mechanical contractor, currently takes a total of four hours to install a residential heating/air conditioning unit. The company's stated goal is to reduce installation time to less than two hours."

- **A description of your proposed solution**—Here you describe the specific product or service that you believe will satisfy the customer's need or solve the customer's problem.

- **The features/benefits of your proposed solution**—In this section, you present the features of your recommended product or service and build a documented case for the financial benefit to the customer. For example, if your proposed solution is the Univac 1000, and it's been proved to reduce installation time by 50%, you'll point out that the proposed solution solves the customer's issue (reduce installation time by 50%).

- **Technical information about your product/service**—Here you provide backup technical information, possibly including photos, illustrations, and schematics. Also in this section, you probably will provide information about your vendors and the support they offer to end users.

- **Information about your company**—If the buyer has not done business with you before, the buyer is likely to want a little background on your organization.

- **References and proofs**—For major opportunities (and new customers), you need to provide some third-party references and as much data as you can to support the claims you've made about the value of your product or service.

As a distribution sales pro, you should prepare a proposal template that can be used when you need to sell, not just tell. Although there may be occasions when you need to include additional elements in a proposal, you can use the bulleted list of typical elements to create your template.

One final aspect of a proposal that differentiates it from a quote is the way you present it. Ideally, a proposal always should be presented in person. If you merely send it in, the customer may rip out the pricing information and throw away the rest. That would not be good news for you.

When to Use a Proposal

Don't use proposals for every sale. They're time consuming to prepare, and your regular customers will be annoyed at receiving a proposal every time they want to buy something from you.

There are six specific sales situations in which proposals should be used:

- **New (important) customer**—If you're actively trying to begin a new customer relationship, use a full-blown proposal, at least until you get the first real order. Remember that in step 4 the customer has to qualify your proposed solution. This means the customer needs to know not only about the product but also about the value of the organization that stands behind the product and the distribution salesperson who presents the value. A proposal helps with this evaluation.

- **New person**—You only get one chance to make a good first impression. This fact obviously applies when you're trying to sell something to a new customer and when you're working with a new person inside an existing account. Perhaps it's a new purchasing agent who's replacing the person you've worked with for the last 20 years, or maybe it's your first call on the plant manager. When you're working that first opportunity, do something a little different to show that you're a different kind of distribution salesperson.

- **New product**—When you're trying to sell an organization something it never has purchased before, you need to do a more thorough job of presenting than you do when the organization knows what it's getting. Remember that you have to reduce a customer's perception of risk whenever the customer does something differently. A number on a faxed piece of paper doesn't do as good a job of reducing risk as does a full-blown proposal that spells out exactly what the customer is getting and offers examples of other people (like the customer) who have benefited from working with you.

- **Committee decision**—Important decisions often are made by a committee. If you're able to make the presentation in person, you want to arrive with more than one piece of paper; you want to look like a pro. In most cases, you're working with only one or two members of the committee, and they will have to take your information (along with your competitors' information) to other people. (This is a step 2 failure because you didn't get to the right people, but sometimes there's nothing you can do about it.) In this case, put a selling document in front of the committee instead of letting your internal contacts do the selling for you.

- **Big ticket**—Use a proposal for any big-ticket item. More will be riding on the decision, and you need to provide additional information. (The definition of "big-ticket" will vary, and you need to know what that means for what you're selling.)

- **Higher price**—In competitive situations where you know that your price (and, we hope, your value) will be higher than that of your competition, provide the customer with a rationale for buying from you. Your proposal will help you accomplish that goal.

As you think about proposals, also remember the five Bs of quoting. You may be asked to provide a proposal at any point in the sales process. Before investing the time and energy required to put together a proposal, understand what kind of proposal you need to prepare.

Step 6: Close the Sale

The final step in the sales process is the close. For both customer and distribution salesperson, this phase of the sale often is associated with a lot of angst. Often, this is because you really are not at the closing part of the process, and that makes it uncomfortable for you and the customer. As a good analogy, compare selling with a marriage proposal. Most marriage proposals are not really surprises. The couple talks about and reaches an agreement on marriage. There probably is even a tentative time frame set before the famous dropping to the knee and presenting of the rock. Imagine a woman's consternation if she gets a marriage proposal without any of the preliminaries, and imagine how much anxiety the potential suitor has in prepping for and presenting a proposal that the potential bride-to-be is not expecting.

In real-world selling, if you've done steps 1 through 5 correctly (and in order), the close is a logical next step that's anticipated and welcomed by the customer. If anything has not been done (or has been done incorrectly), the close will be tough and unpleasant—even if you get the order.

There are no tricks to closing, despite what you may have heard from other sales trainers. There are some manipulative efforts that will work on weak people, but they yield only short-term results, and you end up creating a bad reputation for yourself that permeates everything you do. Think of the image that, fairly or unfairly, has plagued car and insurance salespeople for decades. The perception exists because some salespeople in those lines of business relied on tricks to make sales. Distribution sales pros don't rely on tricks; they follow the process.

You should try to close a sale only if the following elements are present:

- qualified customer
- qualified decision maker(s)
- real opportunity
- qualified solution
- quote or proposal for buy.

If all of the elements are present, the customer will welcome the close and actually may do it for you. If you've been selling for any length of time, you've reached a point in the sales process where the customer says, "Sounds good. Let me get you a PO." Unless you got the order because you were the cheapest or the only person with stock, this is the epitome of professional selling. Your goal is to have a lot of sales in which the customer closes the deal for you.

Ultimately, you owe it to the customer to ask for the order. If you have prepared the customer properly, there will be very little anxiety—and it all will be on your side, where it belongs. The customer never should feel pressured to give you an answer. Do the right things, and the close will be a logical extension of the sales relationship—in the same way that a marriage proposal often is a logical extension of the dating relationship.

The Scheduled Closing Call

One thing you can do to ease the close is to schedule a closing call. The process is a simple one. After you present your quote or proposal, you ask the customer the question, When may I call you [see you] to get your answer? Then you close your mouth and wait for the answer. This is a powerful question because you really are asking the customer if any more information is needed before a decision can be made. (This question assumes that you know you can't get an answer right then. Are you certain you can't?)

If the customer has all the information needed (and you have completed steps 1–5 correctly and in order), the customer will give you a day and a time for your follow-up call or visit.

The beauty of the question is that it takes all of the "curse" off of the close itself and moves it to the closing call. This makes the close a lot easier to deal with for both parties. And if the buyer gives you a day and time to follow up, you have been given permission to close the sale. What could be better than that?

The question also serves as a "diagnostic" for problems that may have occurred in the sales process to date because there is a range of answers that the customer may give in response to this question. Those answers cover issues such as time frame and responsiveness.

Here are some sample answers that reveal how likely you are to get the order:

- "Call me back tomorrow at 2 p.m." Excellent answer. Looks like a great chance of success.

- "Call me back next week." A slight problem. You still need to clarify the exact date and time, and the brief delay in an answer indicates that there might be an issue.

- "Get back with me in a few weeks . . . or after the holidays." Houston, we have a problem. Answers like this indicate there is no urgency on the buyer's part. This is okay if it's a budgetary quote, but you wouldn't try to schedule a close on a budgetary quote.

- "I'll call you tomorrow afternoon." Small problem. A distribution salesperson should be in charge of the next action item. All the customer has to do to tell you "no" here is *not* call. It's a little better if you can get the buyer to set a time for the call.

- "I'll call you when I know something." Huge problem. Sounds like we are not dealing with a decision maker, or you really don't have an opportunity, or this wasn't a quote for buy, or . . . fill in your own blank here. The bad news is that you found out you have a problem. The good news is that you still are in contact with the customer, and you have one more shot to identify and fix the problem.

There is nothing more powerful than the scheduled closing call. As a professional salesperson, you always should have multiple closing calls scheduled with different customers. How many do you have right now?

Trial Closes

As you've been working through the sales process, you've seen that the process has very little about presentations and a lot about asking questions and listening. Real selling is all about the dialogue between the salesperson and the customer—and in an ideal situation, the customer does most of the talking.

If you've been in sales for any period of time, you've been exposed to the concept of trial closes. They often are presented as asking a question like this: "Would Tuesday or Wednesday be better for you to get the shipment?" This question really is a form of manipulation and should

---

PUTTING IT ALL TOGETHER

Some Trial Closes. A distributor sales pro is working with an industrial customer. The salesperson believes that scrap is a big problem in the manufacturing process and wants to sell the customer a product that has the ability to reduce scrap. The very first trial close in the sales process might be this question: "What is your goal for reducing scrap this year?" This question could be asked before the sales pro even presented a product, or it could come when the salesperson is trying to set a sales appointment. In a case like this, the best answer would be, "We are trying to reduce our scrap by 15% this year." This answer would indicate that the salesperson might be able to identify or create an opportunity. The worst answer would be, "We don't have any goals on that." Either way, by asking the question, the salesperson begins the dialogue that helps determine the reality of the opportunity and the chance for the ultimate close.

A distributor sales pro is working with a contractor, and wants to sell a product that will help the contractor do jobs with less-trained people. The first trial close might be this question: "Are you having any problem getting good help?" Again, the salesperson is using a question to see if the process is on the right track. If the answer is, "Nope. We've got more than we need," there might not be as good an opportunity as the salesperson thought.

Finally, a distributor sales pro is calling on a customer who retails product to the end consumer. The sales rep wants to sell a product that pulls several other products along with it. When calling on the store manager or owner, the first trial close question might be this: "How many line items do you normally sell per order?" If the customer doesn't measure or track these sales, the salesperson might have to drop back and consider either a different product or a different way to present it.

---

not be part of selling. However, there is a legitimate form of manipulation in sales: simply asking questions.

Your questions are a powerful form of mind control because they move the customer's thoughts to an area of your choosing. You can get anyone to think about anything by asking a question on that subject. A distribution sales pro constantly seeks to move the customer's mind toward a place where the customer can buy. This is a legitimate manipulation because the customer retains the freedom to answer the question in any way. But the important concept for you to remember is that each question is a trial close. Every time you ask a question, you get a chance to check on how engaged the customer is in the process. This is not a trick—it's an integral part of selling.

Conclusion

By now you know that you can look at distributor sales as a process. From the first step of identifying and qualifying customers through the quote and close, you now know what you need to do. Remember that selling is a sequential process. To get to the last two steps (where you really want to be), you need to do the first four steps correctly. Don't be in a hurry to get to a failure. Do it right and get more sales.

FOLLOW-UP ASSIGNMENTS

1. Track your results over the next 30 days, and answer the following questions:
   - How many of the possible quote/proposal opportunities occurred?
   - How many opportunities did not make it to the quote/proposal stage? Why?

2. Classify your quotes into the following categories:
   - buy
   - budget
   - bid-for-bid
   - ballpark
   - blow-off.

What did you learn from this exercise? What could you have noticed earlier that would have allowed you to spend less time on quotes and proposals that were not "real"?

3. Review your quotes and identify any that should have been proposals. Why is that true?

4. You estimated that you would close some number of quotes/proposals, representing some amount of dollars. Review the orders you closed and determine how you actually did. If you were less successful than you thought you would be, identify the reasons.

5. Review the number of closing calls you have scheduled right now and determine if it is more or less than it was 30 days ago. Decide how many of these you think you will close.

The Perfect Sales Call

Before you begin, answer these questions:

1. How many of the appointments you had scheduled in the last month occurred on the day and at the exact time planned?

2. When that didn't happen, what was the reason? Was it the customer's decision, or was it your failure either to be prepared or to get there/call on time?

3. How many new pieces of business did you find as a result of your sales calls during the last month?

4. How many existing opportunities did you move forward as a result of your calls?

5. How many of your calls were on target accounts? How many were trying to sell focus products?

6. What are the five elements that must be present for a sales call to be real?

7. For a few of your recent important sales calls, what did you do to prepare for each call? What did you do after each call?

The sales call is the building block of the distribution sales relationship. Everything that happens in sales happens on the sales call—whether on the phone or in person. A lot of distribution salespeople take this for granted.

Sales Call Problems

As a pro, you can do some diagnostics on your sales efforts to see if there might be a problem, either with the way in which you try to set calls or with the perceived value of your sales calls from the customer's perspective. All of the examples below assume that you have a scheduled appointment of some sort. When these things occur on a cold call, it's par for the course and may mean little or nothing. When you have an appointment scheduled, watch for these kinds of situations:

- **Customer asks you to drop off the information.** You have an appointment, but the customer is "too busy" to see you and asks that you drop off your information or come back at another time. Although there are times when the situation is legitimate, more often it's an indication that you have not presented the call as valuable to the customer or prospect. This is more likely to occur when you have made non-value-added calls in the past.

- **Customer isn't there.** Worse than the customer who's too busy is the customer who isn't there. In the former case, at least you can pretend that the customer had every intention of seeing you and something more important came up. The customer who isn't in is showing the highest possible disregard for your time. The odds are strong that the customer never had any intention of seeing you and merely committed to an appointment to get you off the phone or out of the office.

- **Customer meets you in the lobby.** A more polite brush-off is the lobby call. You show up for your appointment, and the customer promptly meets you in the lobby (or on the loading dock or some other place). The customer gives you a few minutes and maybe even thanks you for stopping by. Read between the lines here: your call was not important enough to deserve real time. It's lucky (I guess) that the person was nice enough to patronize you with face time for a minute or two. Sometimes, if you do a really good job of capturing the customer's interest, you'll be invited back and end up making a real sales call.

- **Customer makes you wait.** Often the customer sees you, but makes you cool your heels for x amount of time before seeing you. This is a tough one—some schools of thought suggest that you wait for no more than a few minutes before you leave. There are times when this is the right answer; but if you're calling on a really important customer or prospect, you might want to stick it out (unless you have a real sales call scheduled next that requires you to leave so you arrive there on time). Here, you occasionally are dealing with an egomaniac who merely is trying to put you in your place by making you wait. More often, the problem is that you presented yourself as having so little value that the customer did not feel any need to see you at the agreed time. If a particular customer always does this to you, budget a little extra time for the call so you won't be late for the next one. If you're dealing with the latter scenario, and it's one of your regulars, you may be able to train the customer out of the bad habit by "selling" the value of an appointment with you.

Situations vary, and all distribution salespeople occasionally will find themselves involved in these scenarios. As a pro, you're looking for patterns. Does this happen frequently, regardless of the customer? Does it happen with some customers and not others? What might you need to do to create more perceived value in the customer's mind?

The Purpose of a Sales Call

Start with an understanding of what you're trying to accomplish. There are three goals of a sales call: (1) to determine the value of future calls, (2) to find a piece of business, and (3) to drive a piece of business forward.

Goal #1: Determine the Value of Future Calls

The first consideration in every sales call is how much time you should spend there. When you're dealing with a prospect, you quickly must determine how much potential exists—and the viability of that potential. As an example, you might be able to sell the organization $1 million worth of product, but with a few little problems:

- The customer has an integrated supply agreement that doesn't renew for three years.

- The local organization has no decision-making authority.

- All decisions regarding supply are made by a corporate supply chain management group that is located in Sydney, Australia.

In cases like those, the potential is tempting, but reality says, "Let's put this on the back burner."

When you're dealing with existing customers, you still need to make some effort to determine if they remain qualified. A customer may have purchased $200,000 worth of products from you last year, but this year there might be a little problem:

- The business is off by 20% and the potential purchases from you are likely to be off by 80%.

- The customer recently was purchased by a multinational firm that has a centralized purchasing approach, so all decisions are likely to be made in—you guessed it—Sydney, Australia.

- The owner just went through a divorce, and the company probably will be sold. No one is spending any money until the future is more definite.

So, a distribution sales pro always is making sales calls with a primary purpose of determining how much (if any) time needs to be spent with a particular customer or prospect.

Goal #2: Find a Piece of Business

The second and third goals are simpler and are basic to sales.

When you know you have a chance of doing enough business to make it worth your while, the key is finding a piece of business on which to work. If you're selling the customer three items, and you get an opportunity to work on selling a fourth item, you've done your job. Good distribution salespeople pay a lot of attention to this because all of their income ultimately comes from their efforts to find new opportunities.

Here's an example: You call on a hair stylist and discover that although she purchases all of her gels and mousses from you, you get no sales on any of the "supply" consumables, such as combs and brushes. You present some samples of these products, and the customer agrees to try them out over the next month.

Goal #3: Drive a Piece of Business Forward

When you find a piece of business, you need to make sales calls to move it closer to the ultimate "yes" or "no" that defines sales success. A huge number of sales are lost not because of issues such as price or service, but simply because distribution salespeople do not follow up on a piece of business that they have uncovered.

Sticking with our earlier example, an example of a sales failure would be failing to follow up with the stylist to see how people liked your products. Sales success would be scheduling a follow-up call with the customer to review how the products worked and possibly getting permission to quote the stylist on upcoming needs.

Here's a good list of questions to go over mentally before you try to schedule a call:

- What do I need to do to determine how much time I should spend here?

- What's the new opportunity that I will try to create or find?

- Which opportunities can I move closer to a "yes" or "no" answer with this call?

If you can't come up with at least one answer to any of those questions, it might not be a good call.

A distribution sales pro also will ask similar questions before the call is completed. If you can't answer them on the call, the call has not been worthwhile. The only good news is that if you recognize it before the call ends, you get one more chance to make something happen.

The Definition of a Sales Call

To prevent any confusion, I need to give you a definition of a professional sales call. Such a call has the following elements:

- **Definite person**—Sounds simple enough: have a specific person who knows that you're coming in or calling. The problem is that a lot of sales calls don't have this element. The salesperson makes a "milk run" kind of call, visiting a customer every Tuesday morning and seeing whomever is there. The verdict: not a real sales call. Selling requires a dialogue with someone who knows you want to have that dialogue. "They expect me every Tuesday" really is not enough. (We'll build an example as we go along. The first element is at least one individual who expects to see you—in this case, it's Mary.)

- **Definite date**—Huge numbers of sales calls have very indefinite dates on which they're supposed to occur. "I'll get back with you early next week" doesn't count as an element of a professional sales call. (For our example, the definite date is September 13. Now, we have Mary and September 13.)

- **Definite time**—When considering the reality of a sales call, you need to take a hard look at the timing of the call. Has the cus-

---

PUTTING IT ALL TOGETHER

A Really Good Distributor Sales Call Plan. Your company sells plants and associated supplies to a small chain (three locations). Last year, the customer bought more than $100,000 worth of plants from you, mainly bedding plants. Because the customer relies heavily on new construction, your first concern is whether the customer will be able to buy similar quantities from you this year. You have two other concerns: (1) although the customer is buying bedding plants from you, you're getting no orders for the trees you sell; and (2) the customer also is not buying any of your other supply items.

To set up a professional call, you want to include four topics from the customer's business plan:

- How does the customer see the immediate future? (Is the customer optimistic or pessimistic? This helps you with your estimate of sales on current products.)

- What does the customer think sales will look like this year? (Here you're asking a "mix" question by which you're trying to find out if the customer expects to sell different combinations of product than during the past year.)

- What are the customer's plans to find new customers? (Is the customer trying to grow business with new customers? If so, what kind of business? With what kinds of customers?)

(continued)

- Is there a goal to move into new markets? (Is the customer planning to expand into different geographies? Using a different approach, such as the Internet?)

If you are able to uncover any of these issues, you have the opportunity to tie the customer's goals into your sales plan for the customer. Your goal here is to move an opportunity forward on the bedding plants that you currently are selling. You do this by helping the customer sell more.

Because this is an important customer—and you want to continue to provide a high level of service—you recognize that the customer can be a better customer if you simply sell more of what you have to offer. So you also set the call up to discuss

- the customer's tree purchases: How much? What kind? From whom? Why from that distributor?

- the customer's supply purchases: How much? What supplies? From whom? Why?

In this case, the salesperson is touching all of the key items required to make a professional distributor sales call. The rep is addressing potential and creating two discussions in which it may be possible to find a new opportunity or drive forward an existing opportunity (on bedding plants).

tomer made a definite time commitment? Again, "I'll call you on Tuesday morning" doesn't qualify as a required element. (For our example, the definite time is 2 p.m. So, we have Mary on September 13 at 2 o'clock. Still not enough.)

- **Sales purpose**—Too many sales calls do not contain a sales purpose. Based on the definition of the sales process, these six main activities would qualify as a sales purpose:

  - identifying or qualifying a customer

  - identifying or qualifying the decision-making process

  - finding or creating an opportunity

- getting your proposed solution qualified or overcoming an objection

- presenting a quote or a proposal

- closing a sale.

There are hundreds of different actions that come under those broad categories. The problems are in two different areas. Some calls start without a sales purpose. (Following up on a previous order or "just checking in" doesn't qualify as a sales purpose.) In other calls, the customer simply doesn't know the real purpose of the call. If the sales rep doesn't tell the customer the topic, there's no way that the customer is prepared for a dialogue or even thinking about what the salesperson wants to discuss. Therefore, the sales call is not as good as it could be. (To continue our example, we're discussing how the XYZ abrasives worked out. Now we have Mary on September 13 at 2 p.m. to see how XYZ abrasives worked. Almost there.)

- **Customer agreement in advance**—All four of the previous elements are of no value unless the customer has agreed to them prior to the call. Selling requires a mutually agreed set of events. Without the presence of any of those events, there can't be a real sales call. A lot of the discomfort in the sales process is because the most basic part of selling—the sales call—has not been set up correctly.

Here's how a sales pro would schedule a sales call: "I would like to meet with you, [Mary], at 2 p.m. on September 13th to see how the XYZ abrasives worked over the past week." This request has all of the elements, and the customer now can provide an honest answer to the request for an appointment.

The Perfect Sales Call

The "perfect sales call" has three distinct phases: *before, during,* and *after.* You must accomplish specific activities in each phase to get the maximum value from each call.

Before the Call

Remember that you focus on making something happen on every call— mainly, finding or moving a piece of business. These two goals plus on-going qualification should be at the heart of everything you're trying to do. Too often, salespeople set up appointments with only a vague understanding of what they're trying to accomplish. How many sales calls do you make in which you're figuring out exactly what you want to say as you pick up the phone or enter the customer's location? These kinds of calls may work out well, but you have put yourself at a distinct disadvantage by not knowing your call goals up front. The first item of preparation is this: be clear on what you want to accomplish.

Before the call, spend a few minutes considering these questions:

- **How well do you understand the customer?** To be effective, you really need to know what's happening with the customer. What's happening in the industry? With the customer's customers? Thinking about these issues prior to setting the call will enhance both your ability to get the appointment and your ultimate ability to make the sale. Customers now have less time for sales calls than they ever have had. They tend to spend that time with salespeople who try to be relevant to the organization's needs. If you understand your customer's situation and goals, you're more likely to offer ideas that interest the customer. (This discussion ties into some of the areas that were presented in the chapter 6 section on qualifying the customer.)

- **How well do you understand the DMP?** Every individual you call on has some level of input in the ultimate buying decision. Your goal is to determine the authority level and the motivators for each individual. In chapter 5, you were given some questions to probe this point. Review what you learned, and use the information to build calls specifically designed to address each individual's roles and goals.

- **What's really in it for the customer?** This applies to both the appointment and the product/service you're selling. This is the question that the customer is thinking about all the time. You may not have realized it, but you have to make two sales. The first sale is simply to get the appointment. The second sale is to sell your product or service. Remember that the customer has to perceive value in the sales call itself. We often are in such a hurry to talk with a prospect about what we're selling that we skip right over this point—and that makes it harder than necessary to set up calls.

The second item of preparation is confirming the call. This activity is not something that you need to do for every call, but you need to do it for a lot of calls and for every one that you internally label as "important." Prior to the scheduled appointment, send a reminder that contains the following information:

- the day and time of the appointment

- the item(s) you agreed to discuss (plus a reminder of how these items apply to the customer)

- a quick recap of any action items that the customer was to complete prior to the call.

Your confirming message might be as simple as an e-mail to the customer:

Mary:

Just confirming our appointment on Wednesday at 10 a.m. to discuss the x product. You previously had expressed a desire to reduce the rework you have to do, and this product has helped several similar organizations reduce their rework by as much as 20%. You indicated that you were going to try the product in five different applications and that you would have feedback from your technicians.

Is there anything else that I need to bring?

John

In the space of a few sentences, you have provided a reminder—along with a soft sell on the value of the appointment. If you do this, you'll have fewer canceled appointments; and if there is a problem, you're much more likely to get a rescheduled meeting than a cancellation.

How many of your appointments deserve a formal confirmation?

During the Call

With all of that great preparation, you have increased your chances for a successful call. Now you have to deliver on the expectations that you have created. Remember that part of the value that you are selling (and one of the three qualifications that the customer makes) is the value you provide during the sales process.

You need to follow seven main rules on the call itself. Each of these rules is discussed below.

Be on Time. You can ruin a lot of good will and lower expectations of your company's (product's) performance by being late to a sales appointment. Approach the timing of your calls with "military punctuality": if you say that you'll call at 9 a.m., the phone on the customer's desk should ring at 9 a.m.—not 8:45 or 9:05. If you have a 9 o'clock appointment in person, you should announce yourself at 8:59. (The time on your cell phone is the guide for this.) Contrary to popular opinion, being early is not much better than being late. When you call or announce yourself 15 minutes early, you may be interrupting an important activity that was planned by the customer and needs to be completed before you get there.

Customers also have this nasty habit of extrapolating the behaviors of the salespeople onto the performance of the distributor and the distributor's products; so if you don't do what you said you would do, the customer assumes that your company and products also won't perform as presented.

Because some salespeople are not good at maintaining their schedules, they use that as a reason not to set appointments. After all, if you say you'll call "on Tuesday morning," then any time from 7:21 to 11:59 counts. But remember that you're trying to build commitment throughout the process. Giving the customer a vague time allows the customer to make a vague commitment—which works really well until the close. At that point, you have to have a firm commitment; and if this is the first time that the customer has been exposed to your need for a firm commitment, a totally avoidable awkwardness enters the sales process.

After the Appropriate Greeting, Open with the Value. The word "appropriate" needs some definition here. Many salespeople have only one style of opening—they get right to business or they spend the first 15 minutes talking about golf or some other comfortable opening topic. More salespeople err on the side of too much nonbusiness talk, but either of those approaches is the wrong way to open a call.

You may not have noticed, but some customers are ready to get down to business with little or no warm-up (as it used to be called). This warm-up behavior was learned from the retail side of the business—predominantly car and insurance sales—where the salesperson normally got one shot at a customer, and there was a real need to establish some sort of human contact before trying to talk business. For many people in distribution sales, there is regular, frequent contact with customers and no need to go through the warm-up ritual every time, unless the customer "needs" it (and some do). Begin with the recognition that different people have different "relationship" needs. There are fewer people today who have the prototypical relationship needs of even 20 years ago. There is less time for small talk; and some customers see it not only as having *no* value, but also as a real disincentive to spending any time with you at all. Further, time constraints and the importance of some topics make even the most talkative customers want to get down to business on occasion. Gauge your greeting on the customer and the situation.

With the greeting over, spend at least a few sentences on recapping the value of the call. You want to begin the business part of the call by reminding the customer of the reason for the appointment. "Ms. Jones, because you indicated that your main goal was to reduce labor cost by 15%, you wanted more information about our Installatron" may be all you need to say, but you need to open the business part of the call with the value.

State the Agenda, but Let the Customer's (New) Issues Go First. If you ever have tried to tell someone something important, and that person has had something important to tell you at the same time, you know how frustrating that kind of conversation can be for both parties (if you're observant, that is). You don't want to try to create an opportunity or work through a tricky technical issue when the customer wants to discuss the last three back orders. You're there for a purpose, and you need to get that purpose out there, right up front. But then you need to ask the customer if there are any new or old issues that are really important to talk about right then.

Sometimes the customer's priorities change between the time you set the appointment and the appointment itself. If you don't acknowledge this, you might talk right through an opportunity to close a sale by insisting on following your agenda.

When the customer's items are on the table (if there are any), ask if you need to deal with them first or if the customer wants to cover those items last. Often, the simple acknowledgment that there are other items allows the customer to relax and focus on the topics that you want to discuss.

The wording is simple: "Ed, we had agreed to cover the following points: *A*, *B*, and *C*. Has anything else come up that needs immediate attention?" By asking that type of question, you set yourself apart from the distributor salespeople who seem to come with an agenda and bull through it without even acknowledging the customer's role in the process.

Follow the (Written) Plan. You have a written plan for every sales call. This plan exists to help you stay on track and accomplish what you need to accomplish. Salespeople who have only a mental plan tend to accomplish a lower percentage of their goals than do those salespeople who use a written plan. Written plans give you something to go back to when you get off topic. They also can be used as an agenda for your more formal calls. A written agenda is something that top-level distribution sales pros use to separate themselves from the rest of the pack.

Take Good Notes. During the call, the customer will say many things, some important and some not. You need to be able to sort out and capture the things that are important. Issues such as product requirements are no-brainers, as is information about the customer's business objectives or how the decision-making process will work on this opportunity. Good notes also will enable you to write good reports (if you need to do so) and will provide an excellent source of information that can be sent to the customer to summarize important conversations and generate next-step action items. Too many salespeople rely on their memories—and, over time, this mistake costs a lot of money. Learn to take notes without staring at the page.

Get Agreement on Follow-up Action Items. A good way to begin the wrap-up of every sales call is to start generating or summarizing action items. For a sale to be made, often someone has to do something. Ideally, both you and the customer will have some "to-do" items that will help the customer answer the question, Do I want to buy this product/service from this distributor?

Schedule the Next Step. This item tends to be the one that separates the great salespeople from the salespeople who merely are adequate. Simple in concept, it's a powerful tool that a sales pro can use not only to move the sale forward but also to determine if there are issues to be addressed before they become critical.

The final part of any sales call should involve asking the question, When do we need to speak/get together next? Too many distribution sales reps handle this with a statement rather than a question: "I'll call you next Tuesday to see if the test results are what we both want them to be." This fails the test of getting customer buy-in. You want to use this question to see if there are any issues. Asking a question gives the customer the opportunity to disclose information about time frame and sense of urgency. This is important when considering how much time you should spend with a given customer on a given opportunity.

• • •

If you have done all of these things on your sales calls, you have performed at the level required to move each opportunity through the sales process as quickly as possible.

After the Call

When the call is complete, you still have work to do. The amount of work may vary, depending on the importance of the call, but consider doing some of the following things on every call—and all of them on the most important calls:

- **Send the customer a written summary** (and copy everyone who needs to know about the call). After making an important call, write up the notes of the call, and send them back to the customer. Be sure to include the definition of action items and the schedule for the next call. You also can use this document to update other people who might have a stake in the call inside the customer's organization. (The really neat thing about this document is that it easily can be sent to the customer in advance of the next meeting so your follow-up document becomes your confirmation document for the next call.)

- **Update your account profile.** Your goal on every call is to learn something about the customer. If you learn something, the place to put that information is in your account profile. Good salespeople tend to know more about their customers than do mediocre salespeople, and one of the reasons is that they don't have to rely on their memories for key information about their most important accounts.

- **Write your call report.** If you're required to do a call report, do it as soon as possible after the call. If you write it correctly, it also will serve as the follow-up summary that you send to the customer and other interested parties. You write a document once and use it multiple times—pretty good time management.

How to (Not) Make Cold Calls (*or* How to Get That Difficult First Appointment)

One of the most difficult things to do is get an appointment. Getting that time commitment from the customer grows tougher every day. Some of the reasons for this are outside of what you can control: fewer people (who know what they're buying) and generally less time to talk with salespeople.

One way to address this problem is to make your requests for appointments look and feel different from those of your competitors. Here are some things you can do to make this difference stand out:

- **Do your homework.** Put together a list of customers and prospects with whom you want an appointment. Then learn everything you can about each customer so that your appointment request is relevant to what that prospective buyer (probably) is trying to accomplish.

- **Create a custom value proposition.** With your hypothesis of what you think the customer may value, put together a value proposition that helps the customer accomplish pertinent goals. Make sure that the proposition is important enough to prompt the customer to want to spend with you the time required to explore its value.

- **Do a survey call.** Before you ask for an appointment, make an informal call over the phone or at the customer's location. Here you're trying to learn things about the organization. You don't want to involve the decision maker in this survey call because then it becomes a sales call that you may not be ready to make. Sales and customer service people often are very helpful in setting up a survey call. They not only can get you inside, but also can confirm your value proposition or redirect you if you're barking up the wrong tree. These people also may be helpful in ensuring that you know who the right people are—and in getting you past the gatekeepers. If your customers have sales or customer service people, use them as part of the learning process. In the ideal situation, you can help them in turn by providing access to some customers with whom they might need to speak. In this way, their helping you will be good for all parties. But don't be afraid to involve them when you have nothing to trade. If you're selling something that will make it easier for them to get orders, they may want to help you even if you can't offer them something more concrete in return.

- **Send the customer something in advance.** Send a mailing (maybe even an e-mail) that shows you have an understanding of the customer's business, that outlines some possible solutions to problems/opportunities that may exist, and that gives the customer a specific day and time when you will call to ask for an appointment.

- **Call,** just as you said you would.

This isn't a surefire method. Even after doing all of those things, you'll be unable to get appointments with some people. However, this process does have the advantage of being field-tested a few million times—with better results than most other methods.

A Few Rules for Sales Calls

You can sum up the sales call portion of professional selling with a few simple rules:

- **Make no cold calls.** Cold calls normally are bad ideas. They allow you to waste your time as you drive aimlessly around, looking for someone to visit. Worse, most cold calls are a total waste of the customer's time. Do you really want your first impression to be one in which you're an unwanted interruption in the customer's day?

- **Know what you want to accomplish.** If you don't begin with a very clear understanding of what you want to accomplish, it's very difficult to be successful—and even more difficult to know that you have been successful because you have no yardstick against which to measure yourself. Before you begin the process, have a clear picture of what you want to do.

- **Target the right people.** You (and your products/services) do not add the same amount of value for all of the customers in your territory. And you don't add the same levels of value for all of the people within an organization. Presenting your line card to the chief financial officer is not helpful. Present the right message to the right person.

- **Make professional sales calls.** Remember the five key elements of every sales call. Set appointments that meet the definition.

- **Focus on the (two) value propositions.** You know that you have to have a clear value proposition to make a sale. Make sure that the value proposition exists before you try to set the appointment. Remember, too, that the first sale you need to make is the value of the appointment. Make sure that the customer knows why you should be given the time.

Conclusion

Sales calls are the "coin" of the sales profession. You always should spend them wisely. You can improve your sales results dramatically by planning your calls carefully *before* you make them, managing what happens *during* the call, and following up professionally *after* the call. The top-level sales pros try to make every call count.

FOLLOW-UP ASSIGNMENTS

1. Look at the sales calls that you have scheduled for the next 30 days. Determine how many of them meet the definition of a professional sales call. (They have to contain all five elements.)

2. If you're doing some prospecting (and you should be), do a documented hypothesis of the value proposition—both for the individual you intend to call on and for the product/service you are hoping to sell. Remember that you have to make two sales.

3. Prior to your calls for next week, send out call confirmations.

4. After you make your most important call next week, grade yourself on the seven things that are supposed to happen during the call. How did you do? (Get a 100, and you earn a gold star from the teacher.)

5. After your calls next week, send written summaries.

Time Management for Sales

Before you begin, answer these questions:

1. What are your goals for the year? What are you trying to accomplish?
2. In the last month, did you do at least one thing to support each of your goals?
3. How much time did you actually spend trying to sell? Of the 176 potential selling hours in a 22-workday month, how many did you spend talking with customers? What percentage of that time was actual sales time, rather than service time?
4. How much do you understand about your effectiveness? What is your close ratio for all of your opportunities? What is your close ratio for "large" opportunities versus "all" opportunities?
5. How would you complete this statement: "If I had more professional time, I would . . . "?

Effective time management starts with goals. Put another way, you have to start with the end in mind. In previous chapters, you put together specific goals you wanted to accomplish. You know what you want to sell, to whom, and at what margins. You know how much of your sales should come from existing customers and how much from new customers. Other goals for your territory may include making it more recession proof, changing the nature of your contacts from primarily purchasing to engineering, or increasing the average number of line items you sell to your key accounts. All of those are valid goals for a distribution sales pro. The question is, Do your daily activities match your goals? For many salespeople, the answer is "no."

That doesn't mean you're not busy. But many salespeople confuse busyness with business. You get an early start and are consumed all day with answering questions and putting out fires—and occasionally working in a few sales calls. But are you doing the right things? Think about this: If you make two or three sales calls per week on the wrong customers (spending about 2 hours per call on prep, travel, and the call itself), you will waste about 6.5 full sales weeks per year, out of a maximum of 48 weeks. Over 12% of your total sales year will be lost.

There is a real limiting factor here—it's the actual number of field sales calls you can make during the year. On average, a field salesperson can make somewhere between 600 and 1,000 real sales calls in a year. That's an average of three to five sales calls every day for 48 weeks—tough to do. These calls can be supplemented by another 300–400 "drive-by/drop-in events." Such calls have no set appointments, but you drop by, check on how things are going, and maybe hand out some literature.

Add it all up, and you're limited to somewhere between 900 and 1,400 personal touches during an average year. If you're working 75 accounts and 25 prospects, you can touch them in person somewhere between 9 and 14 times a year. That's about one personal touch per month, per account. Top-level distributor sales pros know they can't simply divide their calls in this fashion. Some accounts may deserve a weekly call, and you may see others just once a quarter—but you have a limit. By looking at the information below, you can see how this also may limit the number of accounts you realistically can call on:

- 5 accounts need weekly touches: 5 x 48 = 240 calls.
- 10 accounts need every-other-week touches: 10 x 24 = 240 calls.
- 30 accounts need 1.5 touches per month: 1.5 x 30 x 12 = 540 calls.
- 20 accounts need 1 touch per month: 20 x 12 = 240 calls.

With that kind of level, you're already up to 1,260 calls, and you have covered only 65 accounts and prospects. You might not have as many accounts that require multiple calls per month—and you can supplement touches with the phone and e-mail—but I hope you get the point. Sales calls are like dollars; you need to spend them wisely.

There's a simple exercise that will help you here. Answer the following question: How much time should you spend for every $10,000 worth of sales/opportunity? This is a tough question because the standard answer is, "As much as I need to spend." That's a terrible answer, and here's why: you would not spend every minute of every day working $10,000 worth of business—and you know it. To be effective, you must have some sort of guidelines. For example, you might say that for every $10,000 worth of business, you would be willing to spend one or two sales calls per quarter. So, an account with $20,000 in current sales and $20,000 worth of sellable potential should get about eight sales calls per year. (You'd be willing to spend an extra 3–4 calls to get the business; but if it looks like you have to spend another 20, perhaps you should spend those 20 calls somewhere else.)

With a rule, at least you can make a conscious decision to break it. Without one, you end up spending a lot of time in places where the return doesn't justify it.

Major Time Wasters

Distributor salespeople can't spend all of their time selling the right products to the right customers, but there are some basics that you need to consider:

- **Office time**—A key aspect of being a field salesperson is being in the field. Over time, you can develop a lot of bad habits around office time. Do you start and end each day in the office? Are you always in the office on Monday mornings or Friday afternoons? Do an assessment of your patterns, and figure out how much time you spend there. (No question, you need to be there sometimes—although with the remote-access options now available, you probably can spend less time there.) Get real on how much time you need to spend, and then change some habits.

- **E-mail time**—When you're in the office, you probably have your computer on and your e-mail up. You might even read every e-mail the instant it hits your inbox. E-mail has become one of the major interrupters of our time. Every time you stop what you're doing to check an e-mail, you break the flow of what you were doing and make that activity take longer than it should take. Check e-mail at specific times every day, but don't do it constantly all day. (Don't even get me started about all the people who whip out the handheld every time it buzzes and check e-mail in the middle of a conversation.)

- **Reporting time**—A lot of salespeople save up their reporting time for the end of the day, the end of the week, or even the end of the month. This provides a great justification for going into the office . . . and checking e-mail a lot. The best time to do reporting tasks is during the day, whenever you get a few minutes. If you don't have a lunch appointment, do some of it then. Take a few minutes after each call to do part of the call report. You probably have a few minutes here and there; use them to improve the quality of your personal time and to increase the amount of prime time that you can spend in front of the customer.

- **Time spent on the wrong customers**—This is a big one. Too often, we get in the habit of treating all customers alike. Good in theory, lousy in practice. Some customers are more important than others. In fact, some prospects to whom you currently don't sell are more important than some of your purchasing customers. Use the guidelines that we developed above to help you spend the right amount of time with the right customers.

Tips on Time Management

Some of the best tips on time management for distribution salespeople simply involve doing the opposite of some of the time-wasting activities listed above:

- **Spend less time in the office.** Or figure out a time to go to the office when neither coworkers nor customers are likely to find you. Early morning is a good time. The good news is that you really aren't losing any quality family time, and you may be able to make it up to the family by getting home earlier in the evening.

- **Establish some e-mail discipline.** Look at e-mail three times per day. You don't have to answer every e-mail right away. What happens when you get an e-mail while you're on a call? You answer it later. Pretend that you're with a customer when some of your e-mails arrive. Important customers and prospects get immediate answers; others might get an answer before the end of the day. Make a conscious decision on this practice.

- **Do your reports on an ongoing basis.** Not only does this take less time, but the reports also are more accurate because your memory is fresher.

- **Spend the right amount of time with customers.** Guard your time jealously. Learn how to respond properly. A third-tier customer who wants to see you should be given the "yes-but" answer—"I will be close to you on Tuesday afternoon. How does 4:30 sound?" Do this instead of dropping everything and running out there right away.

There are a few other things that the best distributor sales pros do on a regular basis:

- **Avoid milk runs.** It's easy to get in the habit of regularly visiting everyone in an area. This is great if they're all key accounts. Most salespeople end up sprinkling in a liberal dose of second- and third-tier accounts to round out their days. You might be better off seeing some of those accounts a lot less and driving a little farther to make an important call.

- **Plan your weeks better.** Don't be a "star" salesperson. On the flipside of the milk run problem is the salesperson who drives back and forth across the territory—creating a star pattern of appointments. The best salespeople make anchor calls on key accounts and then build smart driving plans around them, without wasting time in places where they should not be.

- **Maximize drive time.** This is a touchy point because safety is a key issue, but planned drive time can be used very effectively to handle a lot of the customer service issues that might end up putting you in the office. Scheduled phone calls during planned drive time may convert huge chunks of wasted time into valuable time. Hands-free units are the key here. Do it safely, but do it whenever you can.

- **Budget the time for your sales calls.** When you set an appointment, tell the customer your time frame: "I need about 30 minutes of your time" or "This might take an hour." By setting the time frames, you force yourself to do a better job of planning and executing your calls. This also allows you to follow the next suggestion.

- **End calls gracefully.** Hard to believe, but this is a key sales skill. You know what time it is, and you know how long it will take to get to the next meeting—or you know when you're supposed to do your next activity. Pay attention to time, and begin to shut down your calls 5–10 minutes before you have to leave. A good way to do this is either to begin summarizing where you are or to begin listing action items. There might be times when you have to leave before you want to, but this gives you the opportunity to schedule the next step. Calls often go on too long—and this creates a lot of wasted time later. Better to schedule that follow-up phone call and stay on time.

- **Use lunch for appointments.** It's tougher today than it used to be, but learn to use a lunch appointment to see some customers. Some organizations no longer permit their employees to accept meals from salespeople, but many do—and you can convert about 200 hours of dead time into profitable time by taking customers to lunch.

- **Learn to delegate.** Many distributor salespeople do a lot of work that others are paid to do. Maybe there are some quotes that you have to prepare, but do you have to do *every* one of them? Do you have to take every order from *every* customer, or are there people in the branch who can help you on this? You might want to see every order from your key accounts, but probably there are lots of things you're doing that you don't have to do. Too many salespeople end up being glorified customer service reps when their territories reach a certain size, because of the sheer load of paperwork they have to do. Wouldn't you rather be out selling?

- **Avoid volunteering for deliveries.** Some distributor salespeople seem to relish the chance to pick up some part and drive it 50 miles to help a customer. That's a great idea in some cases, but it's a waste of time in others. When your best customer needs something, and there is no other way to get it there, be the hero. When it's a $500-a-year customer (with another $100 worth of potential), find another way. The two or three hours you waste will be gone for good, and you'll have trained a low-level customer to expect an unrealistic service level that the customer probably will take advantage of again, and again, and again.

Basic Time-Management Rules and Tools

There are a few things that tend to apply to everyone. You probably already know these rules, but they're worth restating because almost no one follows them consistently.

The first rule is *Know where things are.* How much time do you waste in an average week looking for something that you need? A random audit of a lot of computers shows me that hundreds of files are not saved in folders. That kind of disorganization requires an individual to remember the file name or when the file was worked on last in order to retrieve it. There's no excuse for having any loose files on your computer. Every file should be in a folder. If you create a file and have no folder to put it in, set up a folder for it when you create the file.

You probably continue to use paper for some things. Same rule. All paper goes in a labeled folder. (By the way, "Miscellaneous" is not an appropriate label.)

The subset of this rule is *Keep good customer records.* How much time do you spend searching for a customer's phone number, e-mail address, or physical address? If you have current account profiles (and you know where they are), you won't have this problem.

The next rule is *Do something with everything you touch.* When you pick up an item, do something with it immediately. This applies to a credit memo, a warranty claim, or a voicemail message. Too many people start a task and then don't finish it. That wastes time and often costs even more time because the problem gets bigger when we don't address it. Make sure that you take a few quiet moments to handle these issues—and finish them when you start them. If you can't finish them because you're waiting for someone else, schedule the next step, create a folder, and put everything you need in that folder.

The most important time-management tools are

- yearly goals
- a daily, written, prioritized "to-do" list.

We've talked about it. Keep it in mind. You must have yearly goals toward which you're working. Occasionally (at least weekly), look at what you said you were going to accomplish during the year, and compare it to your plan for the week. Is there anything in your plan for the week that helps you accomplish your bigger goals? As an example, if you decided that you wanted 20% of your business to come from new customers, are there any prospecting activities scheduled for the week?

A lot of people keep lists of tasks. The most common type is the legal pad with page after page of actions written down, with scratch-throughs or checkmarks to indicate the activities that have been accomplished. Not good enough. Effective time management uses a daily list. You can keep the legal pad if it makes you happy, but go through your list on a daily basis, and transfer a realistic set of activities that you intend to accomplish tomorrow to your "today" list.

Prioritize the activities on your list. The simplest way is to have three categories, A, B, and C. The As should be done first. Probably all of your sales appointments should be As; but as you put your schedule together, try to schedule the most important appointments first each day. That way, if you have a crisis later in the day, you'll have done the most important things already.

During a normal sales day, there will be several nonappointment-type activities that you also want to accomplish. List them in the categories. When you get a canceled appointment, go to your highest priority item and do it. If you still have time, go to the next one. You'll be surprised how much free time you really have when you know exactly what to do with it.

Let your list be the last thing you do every day. Prepare it at the end of the day. Don't ever end the day without creating your list for the next day. There are so many benefits to this approach. Most important, you need to plan your next day when things are fresh in your mind. Don't start the day trying to remember what's important; start the day doing the important things. The other benefit to this is that it enables you to close out the business side of you and move to the personal side of you. How many times have you interrupted a quality-time activity with your family because of a thought that intrudes from work? If you close out each day by scheduling the next day, you can get more enjoyment out of nonwork time because you're done with work.

A Different Way to Think about Time

Every thing you do can be divided into two main categories—*urgency* and *importance.* Successful distributor salespeople recognize the difference. Think about the various things you have to do. Let's see how you might use the following chart to classify those things every day. You'll notice that the chart is divided into quadrants:

	Urgent	Not Urgent
Important	1	2
Not Important	3	4

- **Box 1: urgent and important**—Many people think that this is the best box to operate in. This quadrant is labeled "1," but it has another name—the "stress, heart attack, and stroke box." The last place you want to put most of your activities is here. Human nature drives us to it. Think about high school. If you had a test on Friday, when did you study? Did you do a little bit every day, or did you cram all that knowledge in on Thursday night (or on the way to school Friday morning)? The good news is that the things you do here are important; the bad news is that you are doing them under stress, so the chance of making mistakes is much greater. The worst news: almost every important task ends up here.

- **Box 2: important, not urgent**—This is the best place to be. It's the space where healthy people operate. A sales pro with an important quote to be ready on Friday does a rough draft on Monday and then has a few days to polish it. Think about how this works in terms of your income tax return. If you start to work on it in January, you get it finished and turned in at your leisure. If you do nothing on it until April, you have a ton of stress as you run around trying to find receipts. Do it in January—box 2; by April, it has decayed to box 1.

- **Box 3: urgent, not important**—A lot of life finds its way into this quadrant, primarily because of other people's priorities. An example would be a customer who calls with an urgent request for a quote on a massive project at 4 p.m. on the Friday before you leave for vacation. If the customer is a good one, this is a legitimate box 1 activity. But what if this is a customer you don't know much about, and what you do know suggests that the customer is just yanking your chain? It's definitely urgent, but is the task really important?

- **Box 4: Not urgent, not important**—This is a nice box in which to be. Cleaning your desk or getting the car washed may fall into this category, depending on the circumstances. People tend to be very comfortable with routines, even ones that produce little or no real value. Look at your day, and see if there is anything that fits in this quadrant.

Too much of what we do is based on habit. Good habits help us spend as much time as possible doing important things without urgency. Bad habits throw us into the other quadrants. If you have put together a formal schedule, you probably can avoid a lot of the pitfalls from boxes 3 and 4 at least. A really good planner eliminates a lot of box 1 activities over time. Without a formal plan, you're doomed to be pushed around by your activities, not in control of them.

Self-Management Tools

For a salesperson, there are three primary self-management tools: a target account list, an itinerary, and opportunity tracking.

Target Account List

One of the most important questions for a salesperson to ask and answer is, Where should I spend my time? The answer should be contained in a target account list, or TAL. (See exhibit 9-1 for an example.) The TAL is supposed to contain the names of existing customers and prospects. To make it to the TAL, an existing customer needs to meet one of two criteria: potential and strategic importance.

Minimum Thresholds of Sales/Potential. There are two factors here—sales and potential. At a certain amount of sales, an account becomes important. What is that amount? There's no universal right answer, but there is a right answer for *your* territory. All accounts over $50,000 in sales may qualify, or maybe all accounts over $100,000. Start by doing a review of last year's sales in your territory. Arrange them from top to bottom. Which accounts make up 80% of the sales from last year? Your top 20 or your top 50? These accounts probably deserve to be considered for your TAL.

The second factor is potential. As you look at your accounts, do you find at the bottom some accounts that have a lot of potential? It could be that an account with which you currently do only $2,500 has $100,000 of potential. If so, this account deserves a promotion. Look not only at where you have had success; look also at where you *should* have success.

When you have done that analysis, the second step is to look at the future of these accounts. They may have been strong last year, but what about this year? Accounts can have lower importance over time, especially if you're

Exhibit 9-1. Sample Target Account List.

Account Name	Customer or Prospect	Contact Frequency
ABC	Customer	50 per year
DEF	Customer	50 per year
GHI	Prospect	5 this month
JKL	Customer	25 per year

selling products used in capital projects. A customer may not decide to redo a heating and air conditioning system every year. Make sure you're aware of an account's importance before you make a final decision to include it in the TAL. Remember that you're supposed to make an assessment of the amount of time you should spend working with these accounts, so if your estimate of potential is off, your estimate of time will be off as well.

You make your final assessment by adding the two numbers together. An account with $50,000 in potential and $2,500 in sales may be every bit as important as a customer with $50,000 in sales and $25,000 in growth potential.

Strategic Importance. Some accounts in your territory don't have enough sales and/or potential to justify any significant amount of time, but you have to call on them anyway. One example of this would be an account that is strong for your company and, although little or no business is done in your territory, you have to support the other salespeople by making calls. Another example would be an account that is important to one of your key vendors. This account may be significant for them in other territories, and you have to call on them even though there's little sales potential for you. A third example would be a bellwether account that doesn't buy a lot but influences other, larger accounts. Make sure you think about your accounts in this light.

When you have a formal list of important accounts, it's easier to say, "Yes, but" to other accounts when you need to do so.

Itinerary

Professional distributor salespeople do their own itinerary reviews every week, even if management does not. The coin of sales is the sales call, and you want to ensure that you're spending these coins in areas where they get you something of value in return. Exhibit 9-2 presents an itinerary spreadsheet. On a weekly basis, you should review the calls you have planned and ask yourself a few questions:

- **Do I have enough calls scheduled?** You set a goal for a minimum number of calls that you should make. How did you do, relative to your plan?

Exhibit 9-2. Itinerary Spreadsheet.

Key Items (all should be included in each block):
- Account name
- Account contact, job title
- Purpose for call

	Monday	Tuesday	Wednesday	Thursday	Friday
8:00					
9:00					
10:00					
11:00					
12:00					
1:00					
2:00					
3:00					
4:00					

- **Do I have the right calls scheduled?** On a regular basis, the bulk of the calls that you have scheduled should be on TAL customers. Some calls will be on other customers. Look for patterns. Are you regularly making calls on the right people, or is your schedule a whipsaw of calls all over your territory, without the right emphasis on key accounts and prospects?

- **Do I have the right topics for my calls?** You may be making the right customer calls, but are you talking about the right things? Did you have a goal to focus on certain products? Are those the topics of at least some of your calls? Are you doing the right demos? Delivering the right samples?

- **Am I spending enough time selling?** The final assessment of your calendar should be the way that you are using your time. Are there lots of blank spots on the schedule? Is there a lot of (wasted) drive time? A lot of office time? If so, what things can you do in the future to convert some of this wasted time into good, productive time?

Opportunity Tracking

The last self-management tool is opportunity tracking. You need some way to look at the following:

- new opportunities created
- total open opportunities
- close ratio.

A lot of customer relationship and sales management software programs now contain some form of opportunity management. Even if your company hasn't invested in one of these technological solutions, you need some sort of opportunity management format. Exhibit 9-3 offers a sample opportunity-tracking spreadsheet, with one example included.

As with the itinerary, there are opportunities for review that will help you focus on how you use your time. How many new opportunities were created this week? If you have an opportunity tracker, you can answer this question easily. An ongoing task for a distributor salesperson is finding and/or creating new opportunities. You need to pay attention to how well you're doing at that task. Is your goal to create $20,000 in new opportunities each week? How did you do? If you're doing this consistently, then you probably are doing the right things. If not, you may need to change how you're using your time.

A secondary question to ask yourself is, Am I finding the right opportunities? If you're making the right kinds of sales calls, you should be finding opportunities for your focus products. If your calls are not producing the right opportunities, you need to change something.

What is the total value of your open opportunities? Selling is a numbers game, and it contains a pipeline. If your quote volume declines, odds are your sales will decline also. If your new opportunities decline, your quotes probably will decline. A smart salesperson pays attention not only to the sales (and the quotes), but also to the parts of the sales process that lead to a quote. Many salespeople are surprised when sales drop off suddenly. Most of the time, the drop was happening gradually

Exhibit 9-3. Opportunity-Tracker Spreadsheet.

Date In	Customer	Opportunity	Value	Step of Sale	Next Action	When	Target Account
May 1	ABC	Abrasives	$1,200	3	Deliver samples	May 3, 2 p.m.	Yes

in the steps of the sales process—and it became sudden when there was no more business to be quoted. Track your pieces of business through the pipeline, and pay attention when one of the six steps begins to get a little thin. If you have been finding $20,000 a week in new opportunities, and that figure drops to $10,000 a week, you're likely to see a drop in sales at some point in the near future. Smart salespeople see the drop in opportunities and adjust their calendars to make sure that they do the right things to keep their personal sales pipeline full.

The close ratio may not seem like a time-management issue, but it is. If you track opportunities, you probably will begin to see some patterns. You might find that you close more than 60% of certain kinds of quotes and less than 10% of other kinds. What if you almost never close quotes of more than $100,000, but almost always close quotes of less than $10,000? On one hand, you need to figure out how to improve your batting average on larger quotes; on the other hand, you might want to make sure that you aren't spending a lot of time chasing the elephant when you almost never catch it.

Distributor sales pros know their close ratios and continually try to improve them. Look at the impact on your life. If you currently are closing 40% of your opportunities, and you improve that rate to 60%, you may make 50% more sales in the same time you're spending now, or you may make the same sales in 33% less time—or some combination of the two. Use what you learn about your effectiveness to guide your decisions about how you use your time.

Conclusion

Time is the most important tool of the distributor sales pro. Multiple product lines and the high levels of transactions require that time be spent where it gets the best return. The good news is that as you take control of your time, you end up with more sales, and the quality of your professional life improves because you have to deal with less "junk."

Remember that the only thing in life that is absolutely limited is time. Commit yourself to a conscious effort to make the most of it.

FOLLOW-UP ASSIGNMENTS

1. During the next 30 days, try to increase by 10% the amount of time you spend with customers. If you spent 100 hours trying to sell in the last month, increase that to 110 hours.

2. Write your scheduled activities for next week in the boxes of the following chart. Describe your plan to move more things into box 2 in the future.

	Urgent	**Not Urgent**
Important	1	2
Not Important	3	4

3. If you haven't created one already, use exhibit 9-4 to put together a list of target accounts (customers and prospects) with call goals. Use the chart to guide your call scheduling in the future.

4. Begin using a formal itinerary. Use exhibit 9-2 if you don't have access to a customer relationship management system that includes one.

5. On a weekly basis, answer the following questions:
   - How many sales calls are scheduled?
   - How many are on target accounts?

Exhibit 9-4. Target Account List.

Account Name	Customer or Prospect	Contact Frequency

- Are you trying to sell focus products?
- Are all actions recorded on your opportunity-tracker spreadsheet?

6. Establish a formal opportunity tracker. Use exhibit 9-3 if you don't have access to a customer relationship management system that includes one.

7. On a weekly basis, answer the following questions:
   - How many total opportunities am I working? What is their value? Are there more or fewer of them than last week?
   - How many new opportunities did I add? What is their value?
   - How many opportunities are for target accounts?
   - How many opportunities are for focus products?
   - What is happening to my close ratio?

Understanding Yourself and Others: Building Your Communication Power

Before you begin, answer these questions:

1. How would you describe the customers (people, not organizations) with whom you are most effective?
2. How would you describe the customers with whom you are least effective?
3. What words would you use to describe yourself?

Successful salespeople know how to communicate. That assumption was at the base of the creation of the sales stereotype—the back-slapping, joke-telling buffoon who was all about personality. No doubt about it: Having a nice personality is helpful in being a salesperson. So is the ability to tell a joke or a story. In fact, there are salespeople with little or no real sales "skill" who work successfully for years in sales jobs. The problem is that people who rely on the art of personality have two things working against them:

- Not everyone (including your author) has that kind of personality.

- Personality is less important today than it ever was.

To be effective in sales, you have to be able to add value. Communication is still the key—not just the active parts (speaking and writing), but also the passive parts (listening and reading). The problem is that all humans are born with a set of filters that prevents us from being effective at anything unless we recognize and deal with those filters. John Gray's book *Men Are from Mars and Women Are from Venus* (HarperCollins, 1993) highlights the communication differences that exist between the genders, but these differences are just part of the problem. In fact, every individual really speaks a slightly different language. Mary speaks Maryese, and Bill speaks Billese, and Fred speaks Fredese, even though all are using English words.

Most people have enough of an inborn translation ability to get through the day, but a top-level distribution sales pro really works at this part of the sales process, trying to understand and to speak a wide array of languages. This is why people with charisma make great salespeople: they naturally do more of what most of us do only occasionally.

Seek First to Understand, Then Be Understood

The field of psychology has been helpful to many people who need to understand themselves better. One problem with today's society is that many of us carry the unconscious thought that the world is supposed to work hard to understand us, too. Many people can get through life carrying this misguided chip on their shoulders, but not the sales pro. Put it out of your mind. It's not up to the customer to understand you. You have to take the burden on your shoulders. Any miscommunication in the sales arena ends up being your problem, even if it's not your fault. Instead of working hard to get your point across in every sales interaction, work very hard to make sure that you're clear on what the customer is communicating to you.

The customer communicates in a wide variety of ways, including words, posture, and gestures—and the meanings of all those things change with the context in which they're used. The complicating part of communication is that you receive all of what the customer communicates in your own special way, based on who you are. For example, there are cultures where a grin means that the person doing the grinning is very uncomfortable with the topic being discussed. To most of us in the North American culture, a grin means that the grinner finds something amusing. See how you could make a pretty major mistake by not knowing how the grin is intended?

There is no way you can get an in-depth understanding of yourself or of personality types in any chapter of any book. The purpose of this section is simply to remind you of the importance of this topic to the sales professional. Good distribution salespeople think about their customers all the time, and there are many resources that can help you better understand other people. To paraphrase an old saying, the best study of humankind is humans. Good salespeople always observe the actions of the people with whom they interact in hopes of gaining insight that will serve as preparation for the next similar situation. There's another old saying: Those who do not study history are doomed to repeat it. This is especially true of salespeople who don't learn from their interactions with others.

"All about You ... "

Many of you probably are wondering, Hey, when do we start talking about me? Right about here is the answer. To understand some of the ways that people communicate, you need to analyze the one person you know best—yourself. But knowing yourself best does not always mean that you're truthful about what you know. (Most "mean" people don't think of themselves as mean, merely as assertive and often misunderstood.)

Below is a series of opposites. These opposites define or in some way relate to many of the ways that people think and often behave. (The word "often" is important here because people may act in uncharacteristic ways in specific situations.) Much human behavior has to do with context; but for purposes of our discussion, we're going to assume that people behave in concert with their thoughts most of the time—or at least frequently enough so that we can count on the patterns.

For each of the polar opposites shown below, you'll be given a description, and you'll place yourself along the continuum from one end to the other. Your mission is to be truthful in evaluating where you stand between each pair of opposites—not where you think you *should be*, but where you *are*. Your desire will be to put yourself close to the middle in each case, but that's *not* the correct way to do the evaluation. A very small number of people actually stand in the middle. They are the high-charisma types of people because they immediately appeal to (almost) everyone. Most of us fall more on one side of the midpoint than on the other. Put your mark at the spot that identifies where you are most of the time. (There's a later assignment to get others to identify where you stand between each pair of opposites, so be honest.)

A really important understanding that you need to take into this exercise is that there are no right or wrong answers. Successful salespeople come from all over the continuum. The key is to be truthful so you can diagnose stylistic areas where you might have difficulty dealing with customers.

Here's an example:

Right.. | ....Wrong

These sample opposites aren't part of a personality process. The mark on the continuum between these two specific poles represents the viewer's opinion of the correctness of an action. In the opinion of the observer, the action was not completely wrong, but it certainly was on the "wrong" side. The personality opposites presented below are more difficult to define, but you'll have descriptions to help you along.

So, get a pencil and let's begin.

Introvert ....Extrovert

The first (and, I hope, easiest) assessment is between *introvert* and *extrovert*. These words are often equated with how outgoing an individual is, but here they also refer to how you recharge your batteries. If you enjoy quiet time spent alone, perhaps reading a book, you would make your mark more on the *introvert* side. If you continually seek out other people, even for downtime, and turn on a television or radio for company during rare times alone, you'd make your mark closer to the *extrovert* end of the line.

Now let's look at these two personality characteristics in a sales context. *Introverts* have to force themselves forward in social situations. That makes it harder for them to succeed in selling. The flipside is that introverted customers naturally have a harder time dealing with salespeople who project a lot of extroversion—especially when they don't really know the salespeople. Salespeople who are *extroverts* find it easier to open new doors, as do extroverted customers. It's a mistake, however, to regard extroversion as interest on the part of the customer.

A lot of people have a hard time rating themselves as *introverts*, especially if they're in sales. This is where you have to be honest. Are you an *extrovert* or have you merely learned how to get along with people when you must?

Pessimist ....Optimist

Here we have the old half-empty/half-full question. When you look at a situation, do you *first* see what is good about it or what is bad about it? *Pessimists* are not necessarily negative people—although they often come off that way—but they are prone to first observing what might go wrong or how the situation needs to be improved. *Optimists* are not always positive in their outlook, but they tend to see the upside more easily.

In a sales context, pessimistic salespeople may spend more time focusing on the customer's problems than on the solutions they offer. Optimistic salespeople may fail to acknowledge the customer's pessimism or may dismiss it without really addressing it. Pessimistic customers tend to be harder to sell. The good news is that if you sell them, they usually stay sold. Many people are hesitant to rate themselves as *pessimists*. If you're a *pessimist*, declare it. Acknowledging it will help you communicate more effectively.

Big Picture..Detail

The opposites here describe how people view situations. Is the more comfortable look an overall (bird's-eye) view, or is it a discussion of the details? To help you decide, think about how you plan a vacation. Are you really interested in where you're going but have little time for specifics such as the hotel reservations? If so, mark yourself more on the *big-picture* side of the continuum. If you tend to want to focus on the route of the trip, on where you can buy gas, and on the hotel reservations, mark yourself more on the *detail* side.

From a sales perspective, *big-picture* salespeople tend to gloss over the details. Not good when dealing with *detail* customers who need to discuss them. *Detail* salespeople tend to be boring to *big-picture* customers because the customers don't want to know how to build the watch; they only want to know what time it is.

Words...Pictures

You've heard that a picture is worth a thousand words, but that's true only for people who like to communicate in pictures rather than words. There tends to be some gender bias here because men tend to be more oriented toward *pictures* and women more toward *words*. A warning: there are people of both genders on both sides of this line, so don't assume.

Words salespeople tend not to include things like charts, graphs, and pictures as part of their sales approaches. This works well with *words* customers, but it hurts when dealing with *pictures* people. *Pictures* people can rely too much on the visuals and not supply enough words for their customers who need them.

Sequential...Random

This is another area where people find it a little difficult to be truthful. Few people want to rate themselves as *random*. However, the description fits a lot of people. *Random* people are often very creative—think *artist* here. They don't need to follow a step-by-step pattern to get from point A to point B. *Sequential* people are uncomfortable when they don't understand (and follow) the steps.

From the sales angle, a *sequential* salesperson will walk the customer carefully through the process. That works well with some customers but can be perceived as slow or boring to a *random* person. *Random* salespeople may jump around, hitting the high points. Again, that works well with other creative *random* types but not well at all with the *sequential* folks.

Approach ....Avoid

Approach people tend to be heading toward something. They're fairly clear on the end objective for most things in their lives, and tend to be goal oriented. *Avoid* people tend to stay away from things that they do not like.

In a sales context, *approach*-type salespeople assume that the customer is trying to accomplish some defined objectives, so they slant their sales presentation that way. This works well with *approach*-type customers but not well with *avoid*-type people, who are more interested in avoiding undesirable consequences. *Avoid* salespeople have difficulty dealing with *approach* people because the avoiders don't try to ferret out the customer's objectives, trying instead to identify the customer's pain.

Many people find it hard to label themselves as *avoid* people, even though they are. Are you where you are because this is where you wanted to be—or because you were avoiding other things that you didn't like? Be honest.

Task...People

This pair of opposites is another one of the toughies. Most salespeople assume that they are *people* people. It's tough to label yourself as a *task* person. The simplest way to find your place along this continuum is to finish the following sentence: "If accomplishing a task means that people (including me) might have to suffer, I...." Think about the different ways that you could complete the sentence:

- "...would not do the task" or "...would change the task" indicates that you're more of a *people* person.

- "...would get the job done anyway," "...would get it done," or even "...would do it" all indicate that you're more of a *task* person.

In a sales context, *task* people focus most of their discussions on the job, with little apparent interest or concern for the *people* side of the equation. When dealing with a *people* person, they often appear cold or unfeeling. People who have a *people* orientation often relegate the task to a second-tier discussion and focus on the impact on people.

What truly is most important to you: getting the order or preserving the relationship?

Data ....Opinions

How do you like to get your information: through verifiable third-party data or by talking it over with friends? Although the concept is a little more complex, that's the essence here. Some people make their decisions after gathering data, and some people seek input from others. How did you make your last important decision?

How does the difference show up in a sales context? *Data* salespeople tend to do research and supply as much data to their customers as possible on the underlying assumption that this is needed to make a sale. That strategy doesn't work as well with customers who are *opinion* people and really are more interested in how others in similar positions might view a product or service. *Opinion* salespeople assume that the only thing they need to do to convince a customer is to show that others like the product. That strategy tends not to convince people who need data to make decisions.

Fast...Slow

This pair of opposites applies not to mental ability but to desired processing speed. Some people make decisions—even important ones—in quick time frames. Other people "want to sleep on it." To position yourself truthfully on this line, you need to reflect on the last important decision you made. When you bought a house or a car, did you make your mind up quickly? Or did you flip back and forth over a few weeks/months, carefully weighing every option before you made a final decision?

In sales, *fast* salespeople assume that others also make quick decisions. They have difficulty dealing with customers who move at a slower pace. They can move quickly through the process with *fast* customers. *Slow* salespeople tend to miss opportunities to move business ahead with *fast* customers. They think, There's no way they can be giving me buying signals now; they haven't thought about it enough.

Thoughts...Feelings

This is another tough one because of societal conditioning that feelings are more important than thoughts. Whether they are more important or not, good salespeople start by recognizing where they are on the continuum. *Thoughts* people try to make logical decisions, devoid of emotions. (Think Mr. Spock in the old *Star Trek* TV series). *Feelings* people tend to be more emotional and often will use their emotions to help them make decisions.

In a sales context, *thoughts* people may have difficulty selling to *feelings* people because they either do not appear involved or because the emotions of the customers cause them to shut down. *Feelings* salespeople have a difficult time working with *thoughts* people because the customers appear cold to them. The sales reps believe there's a problem or that the customers don't like them.

Risk Taker...Risk Avoider

The final pair of opposites involves the topic of risk. It takes no risk to declare oneself a *risk taker,* so a lot of people make the declaration. But when asked what they have done that involved risk, the answer is a blank stare or vague mumbling. That being stated, there is nothing wrong with being a *risk avoider.* The key is to know which you are. *Risk takers* normally are willing to risk something substantial in return for a substantial reward. On the personal level, they'll ride a bull at the county fair or take skydiving lessons in return for the experience of having done so. This doesn't mean that they drive without seat belts; just that they're willing to take calculated risks that are outside the norm. *Risk avoiders* tend to avoid situations where significant amounts of risk are present.

In a sales context, *risk-taker* salespeople have no problem proposing exciting alternatives to customers. *Risk-avoider* customers shy away from these suggestions, and the sales often are not made. *Risk-avoiding* salespeople tend not to step out of the box; and, although that works well with customers who are similarly risk averse, it doesn't work as well with customers who are receptive to new approaches. *Risk avoiders* also often are unwilling to risk the relationship for the sake of a big order, whereas *risk-taker* salespeople sometimes will take the risk.

• • •

By reading the descriptions and rating yourself, you have taken the first step toward a better understanding not only of yourself, but also of your customers. As you can see, you have constructed a picture of your key personality traits and your thinking style, all of which greatly influence your ability to communicate effectively and to receive communications effectively.

Strengths as Weaknesses

The final thing you need to understand about yourself—and others—is that what appear to be strengths can end up being weaknesses. As you evaluated yourself, if you were honest, you put marks that were "left-ish" or "right-ish" along the continuum rather than at the middle. The farther to the left or right you made your mark, the stronger that trait or thinking style is for you. On the positive side, this means you can use that strength in a selling context. On the negative side, people who are on the other end of the continuum may regard your trait or style not as a strength but as a detriment.

Some of the examples presented above are pretty easy to see. You're strongly focused on *task,* and the customer is strongly focused on *people.* The customer's perception is that you don't care about the *people* impact. Because that's important to the customer, you come across as cold and unfeeling. Flip the same situation around: You're strongly *people*-oriented and the customer is strongly *task*-oriented. You're focused on the relationship aspects of the sale; the customer wants to get down to business. You come across as fluffy and without substance when the customer wants answers.

Two of your challenges as a distribution sales professional are to recognize your areas of strength and weakness and to understand how those areas might negatively impact your communications with your customers. To be effective, you really have to revise the title of Thomas Harris's book, *I'm OK, You're OK* to *You're OK, I'm Not OK.* This means that the customer's communication style is always the correct language to use. If customers are focused on *task,* you also should be focused on *task,* even if your natural style is to focus on *people.*

Here's a bit of really good news: Some of your customers have learned that they are weak in certain areas, so they gravitate to salespeople who are strong where they're weak. Sticking with our same example, a *people-*

oriented customer may like to work with a *task*-oriented salesperson because the interactions help the customer be more effective. The best sales partnerships are formed where the strengths and weaknesses of the customers and salespeople are complementary. If you can sell customers on the value of thinking about things in a different way, you ultimately win a lot more than you lose.

How to Use This Information with Others

Now that you have a simple way to better understand yourself and your customers, you need to use it. In an ideal situation, you would send this chapter along to your customers and ask them to mark their positions on the lines between the opposites and then return the results to you. Not likely to happen. For practice, you need to do a little review with your current customers. Start by taking your best and worst customer. (For this exercise, think of an individual, not an organization.) For "best customer," the definition would be someone you can get to easily, someone who will spend time with you and is receptive to most of your suggestions, and someone who gives you a significant amount of business. (A person who is easy to talk with but gives you little business does not count.) For "worst customer," think of the opposites: is hard to see, spends little time with you, and gives you little business. (A person who is a pain but gives you a lot of business also may be someone to profile.)

Using exhibit 10-1, describe those customers by placing a mark on each of the trait/style lines. Be as honest as you can in describing them. Notice that the exhibit does not contain words like "jerk" or "idiot." If you label difficult customers with those words, try to relabel them using the items in the exhibit. For instance, a "jerk" might really be a *task* person who just does not seem to need any of the relationship that you want to provide. An "idiot" might be a *feelings* person who does not look at the world through your filter of *thoughts.* (This will not help with people who really are jerks and idiots—and there are some out there on both sides of the sales process.) Too often, we jump to conclusions about who people are because we don't understand the way they view the world.

Remember, too, that sometimes the people we like least are those who are most like ourselves. We may be *introverts* but dislike that aspect of

Exhibit 10-1. Personality Traits and Thinking Styles.

Name _____

Introvert...Extrovert

Pessimist...Optimist

Big Picture ....Detail

Words ....Pictures

Sequential ....Random

Approach..Avoid

Task...People

Data...Opinions

Fast..Slow

Thoughts ....Feelings

Risk Taker ....Risk Avoider

our personalities. The dislike may cause us to take an immediate dislike to painfully shy people—not because they're different but because that trait is something we don't like about ourselves. Sometimes the opposite is true. We like in others what we're lacking. Earlier we talked about relationships in which complementary strengths make a better partnership. Don't jump to the conclusion that areas of difference are always the source of problems. They often are, but sometimes the areas of sameness cause the most problems.

When you have constructed this picture of a best customer and a worst customer, compare it with your own profile. There probably are areas of sameness and difference between you and both of these customers. Are any of the areas different? For example, are you and your best customer both *people* people, whereas your more difficult customer is a *task* person? Are there any patterns?

Sometimes, one example is not enough, and you need to move out to several examples before patterns emerge. "Natural" salespeople do an unconscious assessment of their customers and make appropriate changes to their own styles to enhance their ability to communicate. If you were not born with this ability, you now have an informal tool that you can use. Take blank copies of exhibit 10-1 along with you on sales calls, and begin describing your customers. The more you use it, the better you will be at categorizing people.

Develop Communication Flexibility

As you can tell, one goal of the distribution sales professional is to be able to read people and respond with the correct communication approach. Some people do this unconsciously; the rest of us have to do it deliberately. The only real way to do this is to role-play scenarios with different kinds of people. Remember, you really want to be somewhere in the middle on your communication approach so that you don't start by alienating either end of the continuum. To get you started, here's a list of some overview ideas to consider when figuring out how to communicate with various customers:

- **With extreme introverts**—Start slowly. Don't force yourself on them. Keep your volume at a conversational level. Don't push too much relationship on them early in the process.

- **With extreme extroverts**—Open up. Give them a lot of opportunity to tell you about themselves. Don't appear to be pushing them away.

- **With extreme pessimists**—Don't try to talk them into being optimists. Listen to their concerns. Let them know you are aware of the downside.

- **With extreme optimists**—Share their enthusiasm. Don't try to refocus them on the downside.

- **With extreme big-picture people**—Don't go straight to details. Give them a chance to lay out their grand visions and make sure they know that you understand those visions.

- **With extreme detail people**—Don't spend too much time on the overview. Move to the detail level where they're comfortable as soon as you can.

- **With extreme word people**—Verbalize with them. Give them opportunities to talk out their issues. Don't overwhelm them with charts or graphs.

- **With extreme picture people**—Help them see it. Use the white board, and convert numbers and words to pictures.

- **With extreme sequential people**—Don't start with creative ideas. Begin with concrete discussions of their process and how it works.

- **With extreme random people**—Don't make them follow the process. Allow them the freedom to go where they want to go. Be flexible enough to follow.

- **With extreme approach people**—Help them define where they're headed. They are focused on goals and deliverables. Make sure you understand them.

- **With extreme avoid people**—Start by defining what they want to avoid. Don't force them into premature discussions about where they're headed.

- **With extreme task-oriented people**—Define the task. What needs to be accomplished? What are the action items?

- **With extreme people-oriented people**—Let them talk to you about the team. Get them to tell you their concerns. Make sure they know that you know there is a people component.

- **With extreme data people**—Come armed with facts. These people are less interested in who else uses the product than in what the results have been.

- **With extreme opinion people**—Come with references. Understand the kinds of references they value, and have some that meet their needs.

- **With extreme fast people**—Don't slow them down. Have what you need to help them make a good, quick decision.

- **With extreme slow people**—Don't push them. Build in the extra time they'll need to make important decisions, and don't show impatience when it takes longer than you think it should.

- **With extreme thoughts people**—Focus on the problem, not the emotions. Don't cloud the issue; just stick to the facts.

- **With extreme feelings people**—Take the time to hear how they're feeling about a given topic. Acknowledge the emotions.

- **With extreme risk takers**—Help them be informed. Risk takers aren't necessarily reckless. Make sure that they know the risks so that they can make an informed decision.

- **With extreme risk avoiders**—Lessen their risk. Show them how your alternative is less risky than what they currently are doing or less risky than doing nothing.

The only real way to develop true communication flexibility is to practice with different kinds of people. Begin with an awareness of how you look at the world, followed with an awareness of how your customer views things. Awareness is the key. You have been successful as a human being and a salesperson because of the way you think and communicate. You're very comfortable in dealing with things from your perspective. The customer is in the same situation. The customer, too, has been successful by doing things a certain way.

You won't win every order. There will be some orders you can't win, regardless of your approach. But you can avoid the losses that are based not on what you say, but on how you say it. Identify the differences between your preferred style and your customer's preferred style. Then do everything you can to start in the middle and move in the customer's direction over the course of the interaction.

You also can see that you may need to document (at least for important accounts) customers' thinking/communication styles. You'll prepare differently for different individuals if you pay attention to the information you gather in this process.

Conclusion

In the early days of selling, the salesperson's personality was the key. Sales pros of today know that effectiveness comes from understanding how personalities mesh between themselves and their customers. Start with understanding who you really are and who your customer really is, and then make the necessary alterations to increase your effectiveness.

FOLLOW-UP ASSIGNMENTS

1. Make copies of exhibit 10-1, and hand them out to a few people who know you. Ideally, this group will include some of your coworkers and a couple of customers. Explain the process to them, and ask them to describe you between each of the opposite poles. If you can, ask them to describe themselves as well. When they return the forms to you, compare their descriptions of you with your description of you. How do you come across? Are you accurately projecting yourself, or are you fooling them? Be honest. You may have described yourself as a *sequential* person, but if everyone around you describes you as *random,* guess what? You probably are *random.*

2. If you can get them to describe themselves, you have an opportunity for another great exercise. You should describe them first, without knowing how they describe themselves. Then you can see how accurate your view of them is (if they're being honest about themselves).

3. Make an assessment of your best/worst customers. Determine what it tells you. Remember that problems can come from areas of agreement and areas of disagreement.

4. If you did not get any help on assessing your best/worst customers, add a few more assessments and see what this tells you.

5. Put together an assessment of the customers with whom you think you're most likely to be successful and an assessment of the customers with whom you expect to have difficulty. See if there are any patterns that might suggest a correlation between personality and job function. For example, engineers tend to be closer to these descriptors: *introvert, pessimist, sequential, task, data, slow, thoughts,* and *risk avoider.* Do you have trouble dealing with people like that? Or are you most comfortable dealing with them? Look for areas of strength and weakness as they relate to different kinds of jobs. Try to change your thought patterns and behaviors to work better with a broader range of people.

Presentation Skills

Before you begin, answer these questions:

1. How many formal presentations did you make in the last month? How many informal ones?
2. What were the topics of those presentations?
3. To whom did you make those presentations?
4. What bothers you most about making a presentation?
5. How would you finish the following sentence: "I would not mind making presentations so much if..."?

Select one of your focus products, and prepare a five-minute presentation. Record it on a video camera, and save it for viewing after you have read the chapter.

Effective selling requires good communication skills. There is no substitute for the ability to use both the spoken and the written word. There are two main approaches to communication—formal and informal. Communicating informally might be telling a customer about a product. Making a PowerPoint presentation in front of a room full of executives would be a formal means of communication. The first kind of presentation causes no problems for most distribution salespeople. The second kind is filled with anxiety and, for that reason, a lot of salespeople try to avoid making formal presentations.

Many people put the fear of making a presentation right up there with dentistry and major surgery. To conquer this fear, you need a process. With a process, you simply fill in the blanks—that leads to more confidence, which makes the whole thing a lot easier.

Making a quality sales presentation involves the following steps:

- Know what you want to accomplish.
- Know your audience.
- Define the key points (plus supporting information).
- Put the key points in order.
- Create an action-oriented ending.
- Create an attention-getting opening.

Know What You Want to Accomplish

Too many distribution salespeople try to put their presentations together by creating an opening. Wrong. Don't start by trying to create the beginning; start by deciding what you want to accomplish.

You may choose from the following general goals:

- **Inform**—Some presentations have a goal of an immediate sale, some have a goal of giving the customer needed information. (This might set up an opportunity to sell something later.) An example of such information might be a new environmental regulation affecting the customer's business. Your sharing this information may set up your ability to present and sell the customer a green product later.

- **Gather information**—There are times when you make a presentation to gather information. This kind of presentation contains some information that you provide as a foundation on which to ask questions and get answers. An example might be a presentation on asset management in which you present a series of questions that the customer answers, such as, "What is your total inventory?" and "What are your total SKUs [stock-keeping units] and days of inventory in stock?"

- **Arouse interest**—Sometimes the only purpose of a call is to get the customer interested in a particular product or service. If your organization recently has added a new line, your first presentation may be to introduce the line to the customer and suggest some specific applications, based on your knowledge of the customer's organization.

- **Sell your listeners on an idea**—You might make a presentation on asset management for which the purpose is to get a group of executives to think about the advantages of turning their inventory over to your organization. This presentation varies from an information-gathering one because you want to get an order or at least an opportunity to quote, rather than information you need in order to decide if there is value to the customer.

- **Set up the next step**—One of the requirements of a sales presentation is a call to action. An example of this would be a presentation that hopes to get the organization to commit to going green because of all the products your company offers that meet this goal.

Before you begin putting your presentation together, ask yourself the following question: At the end of this presentation, what do I want the customer to know or do? You should be able to answer in one sentence. If you begin without a clear vision of what you want to accomplish with the presentation, it will be very difficult to put it together—and harder still to make it a success.

Know Your Audience

With a clear goal in mind, you need to do some clear thinking about the audience (or "audient" if it's only one listener). Here are a few things you need to think about:

- **How many people are listening?** There is a big difference between making a presentation to one person and making a presentation to more than one person. A two-person audience is not twice as difficult as a one-person audience—it's three or four times more difficult. You not only have to focus on the people, but you also have to pay attention to the interactions between the people. Other dynamics, such as those you learned about in the section on traits and thinking styles (chapter 10), are important here—and you need to be as close to the center (think communication style, not podium) as you can be with larger audiences containing different types of people.

- **What's their knowledge of the topic?** What does your audience know about the topic? If you're making a presentation on safety to the health and safety manager, your audience may be more knowledgeable than if you're making the same presentation to the maintenance staff. The challenge would be making a presentation to a diverse audience that includes both the maintenance staff and the health and safety manager. In a case such as that, you would need to be simple enough to be understood by all, without boring the people who know a lot.

- **Why are they here?** When making a presentation, you need to have some feel for the reasons these people are in the audience. Do they want to be here, or have they been asked or told to be here? If they want to be present, you probably start with a fairly receptive audience. If they have been asked or told to attend, you might need to modify your presentation to acknowledge, at least, that some part of the presentation may be more applicable to some people. For example, perhaps you're making a safety presentation to the safety staff, and they have invited some plant employees to attend. If the plant people are not particularly safety minded, they might not be interested in what you have to say unless you can tie in safety improvements with quality or productivity improvements.

- **What do they know about you?** How much credibility do you have? If you've been calling on the organization for many years and have a reputation as a value-added distribution salesperson, you may start with a lot of credibility on a wide variety of topics. (Be careful, however, if there are new people in the group or if you're talking about a topic that's new to you or them, because you may have a little less credibility than you think.) This is a key topic because, as a distribution salesperson, you're always greeted with some degree of skepticism. After all, you are trying to sell them something, right? Start with an understanding of what they know about you, and then either capitalize on it (if you're regarded as an expert) or change it by getting a trusted customer ally to introduce you (and thus enhance your credibility).

Define the Key Points (Plus Supporting Information)

Wow, you may be saying, all this work, and I haven't even begun the presentation yet. Right again. A good presentation—like a perfect sales call—is won in the preparation, not during the delivery. So, finally, we're here, starting to put the presentation together. But rather than starting at the front and working through it, start by listing the key points. You don't need to begin at the beginning. Just line out what the presentation needs to contain if you're to accomplish the goals that you outlined for yourself (with the audience you will have, as understood by you).

To be effective here, start with a blank piece of paper and the question, What would I want to know about this topic if I were the customer? You're attempting to put yourself in the customer's shoes. Given all the things outlined in the section above (and given how much the customer knows about you), what are the bullet points that you want the customer to know?

Write down every point. Initially, don't worry about the importance of the point—just put it down. If you decide that it's not all that important, you can take it out. Don't worry about the sequence either. You can spend so much time trying to put things down in the right order that you miss key items you should cover.

Make this a timed exercise. Give yourself 15 minutes and set a timer. For an important presentation, give yourself a few minutes more, but not hours. If you can't document the key points in 15 or 20 minutes, you don't know enough either about the topic or about the customer.

When your time is up, go back and review what you have written. Does it look like you've hit all the key points, or is something missing?

Finally, go back and add supporting documentation to your key points. Is there a study to which you can refer? How about references you can provide? Do you need supporting data from some technical literature? Just list everything where it goes, with the key points you need to make.

Okay, Now Put Your Key Points in Order

With all of your key points written down, you now can put them in the right order. Here are several different ways to do this:

- **By priority** (highest to lowest or lowest to highest)—Use highest-to-lowest order when you're not sure how much time you have, and you want to hit the most important points. Use lowest-to-highest order when you want to start with areas of agreement or of little disagreement so that you can get the audience on your side before you move on to the riskier part of the program.

- **Chronologically** (recent to past or past to recent)—Sometimes you need to use a time sequence to help the listeners follow along. Recent-to-past order starts with an event that just occurred and works back to what caused it. An example might be a failure and the events that were responsible for it. Use past-to-recent order when you want to start at some point in the past and build toward a conclusion.

- **In cause-effect order**—Another approach is to present something that just happened and then build the reasons why. An example would be to start with a product failure and then show the factors that caused it.

- **As problem-solution or solution-problem**—Most of the time, you begin by presenting a problem and then showing how you can help solve it. An *approach* customer, however, might want you to start with the solution (future state) and then show the problem that it solves. You have to listen to how your customer presents things to be comfortable with your approach here.

When you've put all of your key items together in a way that makes sense, you can go back and cut out anything that doesn't appear to help you make your case. Look for things that need further explanation. Are there items that you're having trouble placing? It could be that you haven't selected the right structure for the presentation, or maybe the items just don't belong.

When you're confident that you have what you need in the right order, look at how you get from one topic to another (transitions). The proper sequencing of key points makes transitions a lot easier. Just review the presentation, and see if you can follow why you went from key point A to key point B. If it takes more than a sentence or two to explain, you either have it in the wrong place or you may need to be a little clearer about what you're trying to accomplish by putting the point at that spot.

The final thing to address is any additional information you might need to help you make a presentation that is well received by all. Is it all verbal, or do you need to add some visuals? A product demonstration? A chart? A graph? Some photos? Think about whether your audience is oriented to words, to pictures, or to both; and make sure that you have what you need.

First, Write the Ending

Your next step is to write the ending. Here are a few things you probably should do at the end of every presentation:

- **Review the purpose.** Remind them why you're here: "You were interested in this information because . . . . "

- **Summarize the main points.** You have done a brilliant job of highlighting the main points, but go back and hit them again: "The three most important reasons that this product is right for this application are *A, B,* and *C.*" If you're having a hard time doing this, return to the first question you were supposed to answer in preparation: Are you clear on what you are trying to accomplish?

- **Generate a call to action.** Every good presentation ends with a specific call to action: "To get the maximum benefit from this, your best move would be . . . . " You don't have to be slick here. Just tell your audience what you want them to do. They can always say "no"; and, if you present your information professionally, they'll say "no" nicely.

Now, Write the Opening

You may be thinking, How strange to write the opening at the end of the process. Not really. The opening sets the stage for the entire presentation. How can you do a good job of setting the stage if you don't know what the play is all about? After you have put the presentation together, it's easier to write the opening. And how many times have you stared at a blank piece of paper, trying to get started? If you get started by simply getting started rather than trying to make every sentence perfect, you'll move through the process faster—and that's what you really want.

A Few Other Things to Consider

When you've gone through the process described above, you have a pretty good presentation—on paper, at least. Now you have to get it off the paper or screen and into the minds of the audience. To do this well, there are a few other things to think about.

Audience Questions

A good thing to consider when you're putting together a presentation is the questions you're likely to get. This will be pretty simple when you're making a presentation on a topic that you have covered before, and it will be more difficult on a new subject. Think about the questions because you need to make a decision: should you anticipate and try to answer them in the presentation, or should you have answers prepared just in case the questions arise?

You really can mess up a presentation—and the customer—by trying to answer within the presentation every question the audience may ask. (Sometimes, answering an unasked question actually causes the customer to want to ask more [bad] questions.) The goal is to figure out what the worst questions will be—and have answers. The worst thing that can happen is having no answer for the customer's question. This makes you look unprepared and greatly reduces the chance of success on the opportunity.

You make several different types of presentations. Every time you talk with a customer about your product or service, you're making a presentation. But there are different levels of formality. The lowest level is talking to one person, maybe across a desk. The next level is talking to more than one person. Finally, there is the full-blown presentation where you're standing in front of a room full of people, maybe using the projection system to show some slides.

When you're making a more formal presentation, you not only need to be prepared for the questions, but you also must have decided how you intend to handle them. Remember, you don't have to answer a question the second it's asked. There are times when stopping the presentation to answer a question derails your momentum, so you need to think through the areas where you either want questions or are willing to answer them. Even in one-on-one discussions, it's okay to say, "Let me write that down, and I'll come back to it in a minute." As long as you show the customer that you are aware of the question—and you do return to it—it's okay to put off the answer. For example, a customer who interrupts you in the first minute to ask, "How much does this cost?" might need to hear a little more about the value before you blurt out the price.

Think about this as you plan your presentation, and don't invite questions when you don't want them. Some people pause at the end of every main thought and ask, "Any questions?" Others imply that questions are okay by pausing a little too long at the end of each thought. A pause indicates that you are finished and are inviting the other person to speak. Because some people can't stand the sound of silence, they fill up those pauses with questions—often not what they're really thinking about but simply something to fill the airwaves.

The other point that you really need to focus on is the *meaning* of a customer question. In most cases, a question is a sign of interest, even if it comes across a little critically. People tend not to ask questions when they really don't care about something. The worst response you can get to a presentation is the complete lack of questions at the end of it—unless the customer simply ponies up a purchase order.

How You Look, Speak, and Sound

Countless volumes have been written about how salespeople are supposed to present themselves. There is no one right answer. Appearing in a tuxedo when calling on a plant maintenance person would be absurd, but calling on the president of a company in jeans and a T-shirt probably would miss the mark as well.

You have to make an appropriate impression, given the circumstances. Here are three major areas that you need to consider:

- how you look
- how you speak
- how you sound.

How You Look. It's said that clothes make the person—and in a sense, that's true. Before you speak your first word, the customer is sizing you up and deciding what kind of person you are. Whether you like it or not (or think it's fair), your clothing says a lot about you. The best advice is to be personally neat and to dress a half step above the customers on whom you're calling. So, if the customers typically wear jeans and a golf shirt, maybe you should wear a nice pair of slacks and a dress shirt. If a customer typically wears a nice pair of slacks and a dress shirt, you should wear a sports jacket over your nice dress slacks and dress shirt. If you're female, I have nothing to offer—and my advice would be worthless anyway. Apply the rule in the way that makes the most sense for your customers.

The goal is to show the customer that you're serious—and successful. People like to buy from people they think are successful, even people who dress casually in their work space.

Also pay attention to grooming. Combed hair and shined shoes are required. For men, facial hair (if any) must be neat. Don't look sloppy; it sends an unspoken message about the professionalism of your product and your employer—and directly about you.

Here are some other things to consider when it comes to appearance:

- **Posture**—Stand and sit straight. Slouching is not an option. Even inside salespeople should sit up straight when they're on the phone with customers, because your voice is often a reflection of your posture.

- **Facial expressions**—Have some, but not too many. You should be neither the great stone face nor Guy Smiley. Appropriate expressions convey interest and enthusiasm, so use them.

- **Head and hand movements**—Again, have some. It's okay to move around a little bit. Movement shows interest and helps the customer have enthusiasm. Some gestures are on target—for example, leaning in when the customer is speaking says that you're really into the customer side of the conversation. Leaning back and crossing your arms while a customer speaks sends the message that you really don't care what the customer is saying. Pay attention to your gestures.

The best way to work on this is to do some role-plays in front of a video camera. Review how you looked and acted, and see if any of your gestures might not help you sell.

How You Speak. The way you speak says a lot about you. You don't need to speak like a Harvard professor to be effective, but you do need to speak as if you should be taken seriously. Good grammar, proper pronunciation, and a decent vocabulary are musts. If you speak well, you have the confidence to be effective with a wide range of people. A limited ability to speak restricts the people with whom you feel comfortable working—and that constrains your sales.

The same videotaping I recommended for assessing how you look also works for assessing how you speak. Listen to the way you use words. Learn correct speaking, and you'll empower yourself to sell more.

How You Sound. The final thing you need to consider about yourself is the way you sound. You know how boring it is to listen to someone who drones along in a monotone. Don't be that person. Learn to use the following four tools:

- **Pace**—This refers to speed. You have the ability to talk in three styles—slow, normal, and fast. Vary the speed at which you speak. A slow sentence means, Pay attention—this is an important point. A fast sentence says, I'm excited about this. Most of your conversation should be at your normal pace so that you can use the fast/slow pace tools to help you convince the customer.

- **Volume**—This refers to loudness. Again, you have three choices—low, normal, and loud. A lower volume is nonthreatening and generally is the way you should address people you think are introverted. Loud people tend to overpower them, and introverts don't like it. Louder words convey excitement. Learn to vary the volume.

- **Pitch**—This refers to the "musical" side of your voice. Think choir here . . . baritones and tenors for males, altos and sopranos for females. Your normal pitch is one of those, so learn to use the other tone to change the "feel" of the conversation and move it along.

- **Pauses**—You know what this means: silence. Pauses are important parts of speaking because they're clues that the listener either should consider a point you've just made or should ask a question or make a comment. Put them in where you want them. Pauses are powerful sales tools because they normally force a customer action. One very important point about pauses: when you ask a question, pause until you get an answer. This may be hard for you, especially when you have asked a closing question, but you have to do it. Don't be afraid of silence. Remember when you ask a question that if you're the first one to speak, you have lost the initiative in the conversation. This is especially true if you just asked for the order.

Don't Confuse the Customer

Distribution salespeople often send mixed signals to the customer. Selling is about an attempt to convince. You put together presentations to convince the customer to use your product or service. Four things that salespeople often do may unknowingly "un-convince" the customer:

- **Making a presentation without knowing enough**—Being unprepared is a showstopper. Know it or not, you're perceived as an expert about what you're selling. If you demonstrate that you aren't an expert, you give the customer the best possible reason for not buying from you. This doesn't mean you have to know everything about every product you sell. Sometimes, the right answer is, "I'll get back to you on that." But you must know the basics and not be tripped up by a simple question that you should have anticipated.

- **Not being clear on what you want the customer to know**—Any presentation can become too cluttered—especially for *big-picture* people. You should have a few key points that you present. That's why you tailor every presentation you make to the anticipated listener(s). Making a presentation to a contractor probably requires you to have different key points than those you would include in a presentation of the same product to a plant maintenance person or a retail store manager. Know your audience; know your goals. Be clear on what the audience needs to hear.

- **Holding positions in conflict**—Sometimes a salesperson puts together a presentation that has positions in conflict. For example, the device being sold was supposed to be labor saving, but the demonstration took seven people to get it right. Think about your message, and try to eliminate anything that goes against your key points.

- **Sending unintended nonverbal signals**—Using bored facial expressions, poor posture, and a dull monotone when presenting a "breakthrough" product tells the customer you don't mean what you're saying. If you don't have the right frame of mind to make the presentation—reschedule it. You can't (and shouldn't) sell what you don't believe in.

Think about the topic from the listener's perspective. How important do you think this topic is to your audience? If you have a clear understanding of the goals of your audience, answering that question will be simple. Otherwise, not so simple. Make sure your presentations are both relevant and important. If you make a presentation that the audience doesn't value, you not only waste your time, but also make it much harder to get another audience with that customer.

Conclusion

With all of the things you now have to think about, you're probably feeling like the rookie golfer who has just spent an intensive day with the club pro. You've got a lot of thoughts rattling around inside your cranium, and you're probably thinking, I can never remember all that stuff. Sadly, I've got to admit that you're probably right. So instead of trying to remember everything, pick one thing and work on it for the next month. When you've done it enough to feel comfortable with it, pick another and add that to your repertoire. Presentations are not like driving a car. You really don't have to learn about the gas and the brake simultaneously. What you're looking for here is improvement; and if you practice a few new skills over the next year, you'll get better.

And that brings me to the final point: A fellow walking down the street in New York asks someone, "How do I get to Carnegie Hall?" The other fellow answers, "Practice, practice, practice." And right there you have it. Making presentations is just like anything else—the more you do it, the better you do it. Part of being good at something simply is being comfortable, and most of us aren't very comfortable with things unless we've done them a lot. Watch the frustration of a child trying to tie a shoe, and you begin to get the picture. The child tries, fumbles, gets frustrated, and sometimes cries.

Making presentations falls into that category. But like the child, with practice you grow. Making presentations becomes something you don't have to think too hard about, especially if you're well prepared. Some of the best distribution salespeople make mini-presentations on a variety of their products as they drive between calls. They want to have a presentation ready in case one is needed. A lot of great extemporaneous speakers simply are people who have rehearsed many speeches and are prepared when asked to give one.

Look for opportunities to speak. Volunteer to give a product presentation at the next sales meeting. Be willing to give a report at the next soccer parents' meeting. Actively seek opportunities to make presentations in front of other people. Over time, you'll get better. And don't be afraid of three other key practice tools—the mirror, the tape recorder, and the video camera. Unlike your friends, family, and business associates, those tools never lie. And, yes, you really do sound like that to the rest of the world. Embrace these tools, and improve what needs improving.

FOLLOW-UP ASSIGNMENTS

1. Watch the presentation that you filmed before you read the chapter, and take notes based on what you have learned. Answer these questions:
   - What did you do well?
   - Where do you need to do a little more work?

2. Without erasing your first presentation, record the same presentation again, using the six steps that you learned in this chapter. Play the presentations back to back, and see what's different. Feeling any better?

3. Look at your upcoming sales week and answer these questions:
   • How many presentations do you expect to make this week?
   • What are the topics?
   • Who are the audiences?
   • What is the one thing you would like to accomplish this week to make better presentations?

4. Put together a presentation-improvement plan. Select one topic that you intend to work on for each of the next three months. Put that topic in your calendar as an action item on the first day of each month. Hold yourself accountable for getting better.

Final Words

Most people never read this part of a book; but if you're still here, it's a sign that you're hungry for more. A desire to learn is one of the most important characteristics of a distributor sales pro. One of the worst things anyone can do is to slip into comfortable patterns. Those patterns help us get through the day, but they also keep us from making the quick changes required when circumstances demand. That's why a desire to learn new things—and implement them—is good for the sales pro.

If you look back over the material in this book, you should be able to trace a few different themes: have a plan, think "process," be prepared, aggressively move your opportunity forward, and hold yourself accountable. Each of these themes deserves a final look.

Have a Plan

Throughout the book, you were challenged to have a plan of some sort for everything that you do. Way too many people go through life waiting and hoping for "something" to happen, rather than making something specific happen. One of the things that I have learned is that a number is relatively worthless unless you can compare it to another number. So, you made 7 sales calls this week. Is the number good, bad, or indifferent? You can answer that question only if you know that you planned to make 7 or to make 12. Or, let's say you sold $100,000 to new customers this year. Again, you must compare that number against your target amount. With a plan, you not only can compare actual with planned outcomes, but you also can get a better understanding of the activities required to produce your desired results.

Think "Process"

Throughout the course of the discussions, I tried to get you to think about the process of selling. Thinking about sales as a process helps you know the following: where you are, what you need to do now, and what you need to do next. Over the years, I've received a lot of comments from veteran salespeople who told me they wished that they had heard the "process" discussion in their first week of selling because it would have made the job so much easier.

Thinking of selling as a process also enables you to apply the concept of continuous improvement to your career because you have the tools to diagnose where your failures occur. (A lot of distributor sales training energy has been wasted on "closing" sales because of the misconception that closing is where we lose most of our sales. You know better now, and you have some tools to improve your results.) Don't let the press of daily routines allow you to lose sight of the beautiful simplicity contained in the six-step process.

Be Prepared

That's a good Boy Scout motto, and it's even better if you're a distributor sales professional. Too many salespeople spend most of their careers winging it. Some of you are good enough that winging it works for you, but the rest of us need to do a little better. Remember that almost everything that happens has happened before . . . millions of times. There is very little new in this world, and a professional knows what can happen and has a response for the "normal" occurrences of the day. If you've thought about it and rehearsed it, you're ready to deal with it. Find the "its" and be prepared for them.

Aggressively Move Your Opportunity Forward

Your primary job is to qualify customers; your secondary job is to find a piece of business; and your tertiary job is to drive that opportunity forward to either a sale or a "no." Although you're not supposed to try to move it unless it's time to move, the flipside of that coin is that you're always trying to do everything you can to be ready to move—and to help the customer move. Huge amounts of distributor sales are lost simply because the momentum peters out. We allow this to happen when we're not clear about what is supposed to occur next and when we don't put ourselves in position to move the opportunity forward. You are most valuable to the customer when you're the catalyst for making things happen in the process. Don't ever forget this value.

Hold Yourself Accountable

Much too often, salespeople try to assign responsibility for failure to others—the customer, their organization, the economy, the weather, Uncle Fred—you get the picture. The best salespeople take responsibility for their results. They control what they can control. For example, you can't control the economy, but you can control the number of good-quality appointments that you try to set. The best salespeople spend no time looking for scapegoats; they spend time looking for customers and opportunities. Focus on what you can do—and hold yourself to a higher standard.

• • •

That's it—the final pep talk of the series. Now it's up to you. You work for a good organization. You have some good products (and services) to sell. You have some good customers and some good prospects. Get out there and sell something—now.

About the Author

Joseph C. Ellers began his sales career in 1978, selling office products, for a copy machine dealer. Since then, he has been responsible for more than $2 billion in sales—most of it within the distribution channel.

Since 1987, he has served as the director of Palmetto Associates, a training and consulting firm headquartered in Clemson, South Carolina. In this capacity, he has worked with more than 1,000 customers, worldwide, to help them increase sales and margins. His work has focused primarily in distribution, and he has worked with numerous distribution associations. He also serves as part of the faculty for the University of Industrial Distribution program, held annually at the University of Indiana/Purdue University in Indianapolis.

In addition to his work with Palmetto, he has ownership interests in other businesses and continues to serve on various boards of directors for other organizations.

Ellers also has served extensively in government, holding both elected and appointed public office in South Carolina. He currently holds a commission as a major in the South Carolina State Guard, where he has received multiple decorations, including two commendation medals.

For more information, please visit www.joeellers.com.